CRIME AND CRIMINALS
IN VICTORIAN ESSEX

Also by Adrian Gray
Tales of Old Essex

CRIME AND CRIMINALS IN VICTORIAN ESSEX

Adrian Gray

COUNTRYSIDE BOOKS
NEWBURY, BERKSHIRE

ISBN 1 85306 007 0

Produced through MRM (Print Consultants) Ltd., Reading
Typeset by Acorn Bookwork, Salisbury
Printed in England by J. W. Arrowsmith Ltd., Bristol

To my parents,
whose behaviour did not
inspire this book.

Contents

Acknowledgements

Research for this book was based largely upon the local news-papers of Victorian Essex, a collection of which is held at the Local Studies Library in Colchester. I would like to thank the staff there for all their help and co-operation.

Adrian Gray

CRIMES AND THEIR PUNISHMENT

❧ ◇ ☙

T HE world of Victorian crime was, in many ways, totally different to that of crime today. Very many crimes had motives that are nowadays less common – the choice between starving, going to the workhouse, or turning to crime for example. Much less was understood about insanity, so a number of murders that occurred in Victorian Essex would probably have been prevented today. Methods of punishment were also very different.

Executions were, of course, the most publicised and debated part of the policy on punishment of criminals. During his time at the Home Office, 1822–1830, Peel had drastically reduced the number of 'capital' offences. Following this, executions became less commonplace and many Chelmsford Assizes took place without the judge having to reach for his black cap.

The reduction in the number of executions seems to have only heightened public interest in those that still took place. Each public execution at Chelmsford during the Victorian era attracted large crowds, and morbid prints were sold (the same woodcut served as a block for printing off pictures to be sold at many different executions). On occasions there was also considerable drunkenness and so public executions eventually ceased in 1868. After that all executions took place within the prison walls.

The most frequent organiser of hangings in Essex was the well-known hangman, Calcraft. He started his career by flogging juvenile offenders at Newgate, London, but in 1829 became a hangman. From then on he toured the country, despatching crimi-

The condemned cell. At dawn the chaplin and gaoler would escort the penitent prisoner to the scaffold.

nals wherever the call arose. He was responsible for the last public execution, again at Newgate, on 26th May 1868. Later hangmen used a longer 'drop' than Calcraft in order to hasten the departure of the victim.

The second most serious form of punishment was transportation. This involved the sending of convicts to penal colonies abroad, usually Australia but also to colonies in the Caribbean. The voyage itself, in very unhealthy conditions, proved fatal for quite a number of prisoners. The use of transportation was much reduced in 1841, and in 1853 it was stipulated that it should only be used for sentences of fourteen years or more. In 1867 the practice ceased altogether, largely because the Victorians were energetic in building many new prisons like Chelmsford.

For many Essex criminals a prelude to transportation was to be sent to the 'hulks'. These were old warships, moored in the Thames Estuary and at Portsmouth, and used as floating prisons. They were notoriously unhealthy and rat-infested and were publicised in Dickens' *Great Expectations*. The hulks ceased to be significant after 1856, again because of the prison-building programme.

Many prisoners were sentenced to 'hard labour' and, after the end of transportation, 'penal servitude'. This involved various exhausting tasks whilst staying at Her Majesty's establishments; the treadwheel and the crank were both common in mid-Victorian prisons, but ceased after 1898. Equally unpleasant, though in a different way, was oakum-picking – the unravelling of oil-encrusted old ropes.

THE "GALLOWS" LITERATURE OF THE STREETS.

"The gallows does well: but how does it do well? It does well to those that do ill."

THE EXECUTION.

Public executions took place until 1868. Morbid prints such as this were sold to the large crowds attracted to these occasions.

In the early part of the period there was a network of 'Houses of Correction' across the county, which were used for punishing minor offences (many associated with drink). These were really a development of the old 'lock-ups', like the one which still survives in New Street, Braintree. These places varied in size as can be told from the number of prisoners they held at any one time during the course of a year. Thus in 1838 the maximum at Halstead was 16, at Newport 5, and Ilford (which was considered a gaol) 39. There was also a 'gaol' at Colchester, which averaged about forty inmates at a time; it was closed in 1850.

All these criminals were processed through a complex legal system that operated at several levels. At the most local level, and dealing with many minor offences, were the Magistrates and then the Petty Sessions which met in several places that would be considered of little importance today – Castle Hedingham, for example. Then came the Essex Quarter Sessions and, meeting once or twice a year during the Victorian period, the Assizes which were held at Chelmsford; the latter dealt with all major crimes such as murder.

An idea of how attitudes to crime and punishment changed during the Victorian Age can be gained by looking at the results of three Assize sessions:

Essex Summer Assize, 1847

Thomas Newport	Encouraging woman to have abortion	Discharged
John Atkins (27)	Arson of barn at Dunmow	10 yrs transp.
George Wood (17)	Highway robbery of 6d. and wounding at Mucking	10 yrs transp.
Josiah Bateman (19)	Burglary at Chappel	10 yrs transp.
Elizabeth Hume (24)	Attempted murder of husband	Life transp.
Allen Richardson (40)	Burglary at Felsted	7 yrs transp.
Stephen Griggs (30)	Arson at Stansted M.	Life transp.
James Willsmore (17)	Wilful Murder at Rochford	Death
Elias Hawes (36)	Arson at Burnham	Life transp.

Essex Summer Assize, 1863

Francis King	Stealing a horse	14 yrs penal serv.
Peter Campbell (79)	Setting fire to haystack	Acquitted
Thomas Cox (34)	Attempted murder	Acquitted
William Wootton (29)	Stealing 58 postage stamps	4 yrs penal serv.
William Abrahart (24)	Assault and Robbery	15 yrs penal serv.
William Harborn (56)	Rape of child at Moulsham	Penal serv. life
Charles Minter (22)	Rape of child at Colchester	10 yrs penal serv.

James Wilson (23)	Attempted murder at Gt Waltham	12m hard labour
Edward Whiting (22)	Stealing £2-1-7½ at Orsett	18m hard labour
Henry Brooks (42)	Manslaughter at Chelmsford	12m hard labour
Richard Mills (17)	Unnatural offence at Horkesley	12m hard labour

Essex Summer Assize, 1892

George Dennison (59)	Burglary at Horndon	Reserved
William Sprodburg (20)	Stole watch at Lit. Warley	Deferred
Mary Donovan (27)	Stole clothes from washing-line at Shoebury	5 wks hard lab.
Patrick Lannon (21)	Window smashing at Colchester	3m hard labour
Elizabeth Ramsay (57)	Attempted murder of husband at Springfield	Lunatic
James Clark (34)	Counterfeit coin at Earl's Colne	Deferred

Some of the crimes referred to in this list can still be found in our courts today, but some have become very rare. What exactly these crimes were, how they happened, and why some of them have died out will be explained in the following chapters.

'WILFUL MURDER'

I T is common in the 1980s to hear people talking about how violent life has become, but it is an undoubted fact that sudden death was far more common during the Victorian Age than it is now. Essex local papers of the time were regularly filled with details of violent deaths in the home, in the street, and especially around the pub. Crimes of violence were common, with many criminals showing a total disregard for the lives of their victims. Yet the courts of Victorian Essex often showed remarkable liberality in deciding whether a crime should be classed as 'Wilful Murder', a capital offence, or manslaughter. This was a crucial distinction, because a conviction for wilful murder carried an automatic death penalty, whereas manslaughter could be punished in a whole variety of ways that allowed the judge considerable room for personal discretion. In some parts of the country juries were notoriously reluctant to convict on a charge of wilful murder.

Trials for murder took place at the Essex Assizes which were usually held twice a year in Chelmsford; occasionally a third Assize was held in December if the business warranted it. Up until the end of 1866 convicted murderers were executed in public in Chelmsford; these sad events often attracted huge crowds, and it was the appalling behaviour of these crowds that eventually resulted in the executions being moved within the prison walls.

During the Victorian era 'Wilful Murder' was the only offence for which people were hanged in Chelmsford. Until the 1820s there had been a large number of offences for which the capital punishment was prescribed, but Sir Robert Peel introduced many reforms during his time at the Home Office in the 1820s; transportation replaced execution in many cases. By the time Queen

Victoria ascended the throne in 1837, executions had become a rarity in Chelmsford; already they had fallen from 43 in 1820 to a mere 11 in 1824, and the decline continued. In England and Wales as a whole only 6 people were executed in 1838, compared to 114 in 1821. In some years there were no executions at all in Chelmsford.

There were a number of reasons why violent death was comparatively commonplace in Victorian Essex. Undoubtedly drink was one factor. A number of these frightful incidents occurred in remote villages, so it may have been that continual inbreeding exacerbated congenital problems. Perhaps the major factor was the considerable ignorance about mental illness, leading to a high proportion of murderers being acquitted on the grounds of insanity.

The cases described below are a selection of the most interesting and more typical murders of the period.

1. Clavering: the 'murder capital' of Essex

It is symptomatic of the pattern of crime in Victorian Essex that the place to achieve the greatest notoriety was not some den of

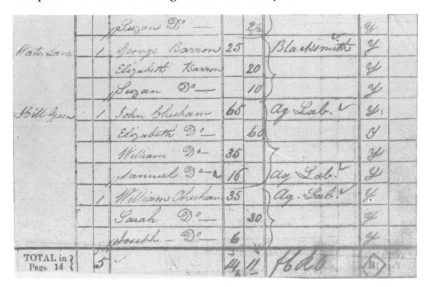

The record of Sarah Chesham's family in the 1841 Census Enumerator's Book. It reveals a life of overcrowding and poverty of the agricultural labourers. In her case it led to the murder of her two sons, for which she was hanged.

underworld brigands, but an otherwise quiet and obscure village in the north-western corner of the county. The tiny settlement of Clavering witnessed 4 major murder scandals during the Victorian years, together with a number of other unfortunate incidents.

In January 1847 Essex was rocked by the news of sensational child poisonings in the district of Clavering and Manuden, not far from Saffron Walden. Sarah Chesham, the mother of the two dead boys, was arrested, with the scandal being given a further twist when a local farmer, Thomas Newport, was also implicated.

Sarah Chesham's life story is full of wickedness and eventually this led her to the gallows. She came from a family of labourers. She was a married woman with several children, but seems to have been unfaithful to her husband and she was known to have had an affair with the local farmer, Newport. Her sons, Joseph and James Chesham, both developed similar illnesses during the winter of 1846–7. Both boys suffered violent stomach pains and Joseph was sick so profusely that the vomit trickled through the floor onto the table of the lodgers who lived beneath them. They both died soon afterwards.

Post-mortem investigation soon revealed traces of arsenic in the stomachs of the boys and the village of Clavering was shocked when their mother, Sarah Chesham, was arrested. She then attempted to defend herself by accusing Thomas Newport, who some alleged was her lover, of instigating the murders. Joseph, who was 10 years old, had previously been in service with farmer Newport.

In March 1847 Sarah Chesham was brought to trial in Chelmsford. Evidence was brought to show that arsenic had been obtained from a local dealer on the grounds that it was needed for killing rats; this was far from conclusive though, as country cottages were plagued with rats and arsenic was in common use as a rat-poison. Sufficient evidence was produced to show that the children had died from poisoning, but there was no proof as to who had administered the fatal dose. Chesham maintained relentlessly that others had done the foul deed. The Chelmsford jury, hesitating to pronounce a 'guilty' verdict where the death penalty would certainly have resulted, acquitted Sarah Chesham due to lack of evidence. It was to be a fatal error.

Thomas Newport did not have an easy time either, for in July 1847 he was charged with inciting Sarah Chesham to have an abortion, but the case was discharged.

There was considerable surprise when Chesham was acquitted for she had behaved in a fairly odious manner and public opinion was against her. She might, however, have disappeared back into obscurity had not the whole affair taken a new and even more shocking turn a few years later.

In May 1850 Sarah Chesham's husband, Richard, died after an illness of several months that had caused him to suffer 'vomiting and purging', together with intense bowel pains. The circumstances of his death alerted local opinion and the surgeon noticed that Richard Chesham's symptoms were very similar to those of poisoning. This time there was to be no hesitation in collecting evidence; the Police visited the Chesham's house on the outskirts of Clavering, and took away food samples that included a bag of rice. The rice, and the contents of Richard Chesham's stomach, were examined by Professor Taylor. He found no food in the stomach, but discovered traces of arsenic. The bag of rice yielded 16 grains of arsenic, enough to taint all the rice in the bag.

Richard Chesham, who was only 45 years old, had died after an illness that had lasted several months. During the last six days of

The area of Clavering where the Chesham family lived. In Victorian times houses like this were home to several poor families.

his life he had been too weak to feed himself, and his wife had fed him on flour and milk. Clearly she would have had ample opportunity to poison him.

Sarah Chesham appeared in court for the second time at the Lent Assizes in March 1851, accused of administering poison with intent to murder. This time her reputation must have counted against her, especially when Hannah Phillips gave evidence. Mrs Phillips said that Sarah Chesham still blamed others for the death of her children but had openly admitted to having poisoned the child of Lydia Taylor. Phillips said that Mrs Chesham had also told her how to bake a pie that would kill her husband.

The trial lasted eight hours and this time the verdict was 'Guilty'. Then the judge declared the sentence of death, colourfully described by the reporter of the *Essex Standard*:

> 'During the delivery of this brief but impressive charge, his lordship was so affected that he could scarcely proceed; and when the prisoner was removed many ladies sitting upon the bench were bathed in tears.'

At the same Assize, another murderer named Drory was also condemned to death. The prospect of a double execution in Chelmsford enthralled the county. Drory became very penitent but Sarah Chesham appeared to be utterly unchanged by the prospect of her imminent death. She spent her last days blaming the family poisonings on others, reckoning that her husband's medical attendant had caused his death, though she admitted other poisonings. Up until her last night she refused to accept any blame and turned the chaplain away. The night before her execution seems to have had a telling effect, however, for she '. . . passed a restless night, and threw herself upon her bed in an agony of distress, every limb trembling with agitation.'

Sarah Chesham was executed on 25th March, 1851. A crowd of over 10,000 people, mostly women, watched as she was carried to the scaffold. She was apparently in such an agitated state that she had lost control over her own limbs. Hangman Calcraft covered her face, and that of Drory, then the drop fell. Drory appeared to die instantly, but Chesham 'struggled considerably for two or three minutes'.

Because of a legal technicality, Sarah Chesham's body was allowed to be taken back to Clavering for burial: most murderers were buried within the walls of Chelmsford Gaol. But the bizarre story did not end there; her corpse was denied entry to the local churchyard and so was given temporary burial by friends. From this shallow grave it was soon stolen, presumably by the morbidly curious.

Only a few years were to pass before the next horrific events in the Clavering district, this time at the small hamlet of Starlings Green. The bare facts of the case were shocking enough, but as evidence emerged it soon became apparent that this was a type of murder that was all too common in Victorian England.

Late in 1861 Samuel Law, a 27 year old family man, was sentenced to one month in Hertford Gaol for breaking a gate. His wife Rebecca and their two children spent Christmas in the Saffron Walden Union workhouse; she was 24 and had already had four children, though two of these had died in infancy. In early January 1862, Samuel Law was released from prison and went to the workhouse the following Sunday to collect his wife and their two children; then they went back to their cottage at Starlings Green.

Starlings Green today is a tranquil spot. But here in 1861 Rebecca Law killed her husband and child in a quite horrific manner.

Four days passed in relative quiet before Rebecca Law woke her parents at 1 o'clock in the morning, by battering on the door at their house at Langley Green. What Rebecca told her parents led them to summon the Police from Newport, and Rebecca was taken to the Police station there. It emerged that she had attacked her husband while he was asleep in bed, chopping his head to pieces with a bill-hook; then, in a frenzy, she had battered 16 week old Alfred, who lay on a little corner bed. It was later discovered that she had used her hammer to murder the baby. She had apparently intended to drown the other child, but mercifully it survived her onslaught.

A local person, William Codlin, was one of the first on the scene and he described what he found: 'I walked into the room and saw a quantity of blood on the floor and on the kneading-trough, coming through the floor of an upstairs room.' He went upstairs to find the source of the blood and there found Samuel Law sprawled across the bedroom floor, with many cuts about his body. The baby he found dead in the corner.

Shortly afterwards one of the Newport Constables arrived at the house with Rebecca herself and the woman openly admitted that she was guilty. 'Poor Sam is gone,' she told the Constable, 'I did it. I chopped him with the chopper. Oh dear! I'm lost for ever.'

There seemed to be no motive for the crime, but gradually the sad truth emerged. Rebecca said that she had had a vision, three months earlier, in which she had seen murder and heard shrieks in the house. She went on to claim that her husband had mistreated her and threatened to kill her, though this did not explain why she had intended to murder both her children as well. A local surgeon, however, observed that Rebecca Law was 'of weak intellect'.

She was tried at the Essex Lent Assizes of March 1862. The jury had no difficulty in recording a verdict of not guilty due to insanity, so Rebecca Law was to be detained indefinitely. Her case shows how knowledge of mental illness was very restricted at this time and was not understood at all in many rural areas; cases like those of Rebecca Law can be found throughout Victorian Britain, and are fortunately far less frequent today.

The last of the Victorian murders at Clavering concerned Samuel or Herbert Dougall who bought Coldhams Farm in 1899. He moved there with a middle-aged heiress, who provided him with all his money but was rarely seen in public. Dougall renamed

Clavering, where in the late 19th century a Mr Dougall murdered an heiress, hid her body and continued to draw on her bank account.

his property Moat Farm and began to mix with the local gentry, some seeing him as the 'Squire' of Clavering. He became a keen supporter of the village cricket team and gained a reputation as something of a ladies' man. The heiress, Miss Holland, appeared to lead the life of a recluse and was not seen again in public after 1899. Dougall continued to draw on her bank account for another two years, however. It was only after persistent rumour about what had happened to her that Police were forced to intervene; a search of the grounds revealed the body of Miss Holland, killed at some unknown date. The murder caused a great sensation because of the high social class of Dougall and Miss Holland.

2. Mountnessing, 1838: A Frustrated Lover

It is generally true to say that most murders are actually committed by persons known by or related to the victim. A number of Essex murders have involved love affairs that went wrong, and the murder of Susanna Playle at Mountnessing on 28th November 1838 was just such a case.

Susanna Playle was a woman of mature years who was married to an innkeeper at Mountnessing. She had had several children, and when her husband died decided to continue to run the inn. A local man, Abraham Hilliard, had known the Playles for some time and helped with the inn after the death of Mr Playle. Hilliard seems to have developed an affection towards the widow; as the owner of a successful business, she would have made a good wife for any man.

Mrs Playle, though, had no romantic interest in Hilliard; he continued to pester her, but soon his pleas turned to threats, especially when he had had too much to drink. Susanna Playle began to be afraid, and summoned her son John home to protect her. He was an itinerant preacher. Not long after he had returned home, John Playle overheard a row between his mother and Hilliard. 'Never let me see your face again', Mrs Playle had shouted at Hilliard. The man had replied angrily. 'Damn you,' he said, 'if you do not have me you shall not have any man.' But Mrs Playle had retorted by telling him, 'I will, I will be married before a month.'

If John Playle had acted on hearing this threat to his mother, she might have lived, but shortly afterwards he came out of the back of the inn and witnessed Hilliard shoot his mother dead in the bakehouse. John Playle was only able to leap on Hilliard, grab the gun, and knock him to the ground. He was too late to save his mother.

Abraham Hilliard was condemned to death in March 1839. Before his execution he spoke to a few friends and warned them about the dangers of drunkenness and Sabbath-breaking. Then he was taken out to the scaffold, with a crowd of 2–3,000 waiting. His last words, which he spoke faintly, were, 'Goodbye, goodbye all; I hope I shall meet you in heaven.'

3. Wix, 1848: Murder for Money

The execution of Mary May at Chelmsford in August 1848 attracted a lot of attention. It was the first execution in the town for 9 years and the first of a woman for 44 years. It was another case in which arsenic was used to dispose of a relative, but the callous manner in which the crime was committed shocked the county.

Mary May and her family lived at Wix, in the northern part of Essex. She was a married woman but allowed one of her brothers, William Constable, to lodge in her house. Constable was a pedlar but he stayed at home when work was available and in 1848 he was working in a field not far from Mary May's house when he was struck down by pain and sickness. In an age when medical treatment for the poor was very basic, no-one had any suspicions about Constable's sudden illness and when he died he was quietly buried.

Shortly after the burial, extra evidence began to come to light that led to Constable's body being exhumed and medically examined in greater detail. It was discovered that Mary May had entered her name, and her brother's, in a burial club very shortly before the latter died. In doing this she had lied about their ages as both of them were over the maximum age which the club had set for new members. Although Mary May was 38, she had put herself down as 29. The burial club was a form of life insurance; if a member died, then a sum of money was paid to the nearest relative to cover funeral costs with a little left over. The fact that Constable had died so suddenly after having had life insurance taken out for him immediately aroused suspicion.

Chemical analysis of the exhumed body revealed that it contained ten grains of arsenic; it was claimed that three grains were enough to kill a normal person. Mary May was arrested and tried at the Summer Assize of 1848. Throughout she protested that she was innocent, but she was proved to have lied about several things, including the nature of her brother's illness. She was found to be guilty, and the judge declared a sentence of death. 'I didn't do it', she protested to the court, but it was too late.

There was a month's delay between her trial and her execution. During this time a petition was raised for a commutation of her sentence, but although 1,400 signatures were gathered it was to no avail. Her behaviour whilst in prison cannot have done her chances any good, since she consistently exhibited a 'sullen demeanour' and refused to talk to the chaplain. She was moved from Chelmsford gaol to the gaol at Springfield; on arrival there she emitted a piercing shriek and threw a fainting fit.

To the last Mary May denied being guilty. Instead she pointed the finger at a man named Simpson, who had also been a lodger in her house. In a typical outburst of anger, she declared that she would tear Simpson's heart out if she ever got hold of him. She also threatened her husband, telling the poor man that she would come back to haunt him if he ever dared to get married again; she instructed him to wear mourning clothes for at least two years after her execution.

Mary May was executed at 9 o'clock on a Monday morning in August 1848, on a swaffold erected above the entrance of the gaol. The chapel bell tolled in the background as a crowd of 3–4,000 gathered. She refused to confess right up to the last moment. Then Mary May was brought to the platform, groaning, 'Save me, save me, where's my loving husband?' But it was too late for anyone to help her as Executioner Calcraft went about his work. Mary May's last words were, 'Good bye; may the Lord have mercy on my soul.'

The jury had not seemed to be in any doubt about the guilt of Mary May, but the resolute refusal to confess was unusual. Yet it is interesting to compare the trial of May with the first trial of Sarah Chesham; one was convicted, the other freed. The raising of a petition in May's favour indicates that there was a feeling in the county that the death penalty was not always suitable, but it was to be over a century before capital punishment ceased.

After being left to hang in the wind for one hour, Mary May's corpse was cut down and her case was largely forgotten.

4. Doddinghurst, 1851: Crime of Passion

Certain murders attracted far more public attention than others. The key elements appear to have been some romantic interest, a murderer from amongst the 'better' classes, and a handsome young man to attract the women who flocked to murder trials and executions. All these factors combined in the case of Thomas Drory.

On the day set for the trial of Thomas Drory, accused of murdering Jael Denny, Chelmsford was packed. As the 'Essex Standard' reported:

'The trial of this case excited the most absorbing interest; and Friday morning having been fixed for it to take place the Shire Hall outside had very much the appearance of a besieged citadel; and the javelin men's staves had to be used pretty freely to keep back the hundreds of spectators anxious to obtain admission.'

The crowd was so densely packed around the building that it took the poor jury half an hour to get into the building. To add insult to injury the judge then complained about their conduct until he was

Brick House Farm, Doddinghurst, home of Thomas Drory who was hanged for murder in 1851. The house has been altered considerably since that date.

made fully aware of the situation outside. Drory was certainly the type of murderer to attract interest for he was quite rich, from a respectable farming family, and also a 'youthful, well-looking man'.

Drory, aged 23, ran Brick House Farm at Doddinghurst near Brentwood. He was accused of murdering a 20 year old local girl, Jael Denny, who was eight months pregnant at the time of her death. Jael's stepfather was a labourer on Drory's farm and for a time her mother had been his housekeeper, so for a while all four had lived together under one roof. During this time Jael 'formed an intimacy' with Drory. Unproven rumours alleged that she was keeping company with other men as well, and it was claimed that she performed 'dances' in the back rooms of various pubs in the district.

Early in 1850 the girl became pregnant, though Drory was later able to produce a note signed by the girl saying that he was not the father. Some alleged that Drory had persuaded the girl to write this note by giving her £10.

During the summer of 1850, Jael Denny and her parents moved

out of Brick House Farm and went to live in a cottage nearby. On 3rd September Drory had a row with Jael's mother, who had heard that he was planning to marry another woman. 'Thomas, I hear you are going to marry Miss Giblin,' she said, 'you will not be such a villain as that when my daughter is seven months gone in the family way.'

Clearly Jael's mother believed that Drory was responsible for her daughter's pregnancy, and Drory's subsequent behaviour certainly suggests that he felt implicated. Later in September Drory produced the signed note, which he apparently obtained from underneath Jael's bed in mysterious circumstances! He claimed that he had not been 'keeping company' with her for the last nine or ten months. At the same time he began to tell people that he feared the girl might attempt suicide; at his trial he claimed that Jael's mother had asked him to hide away all his razors as a precaution. He had also told a friend, George Nickolls, about the suicide possibility; but Nickolls was an astute man and warned Drory against doing anything rash.

Jael died on the evening of 12th October 1850. She had met Drory briefly at 5pm that day, but had then gone home to tea. During the meal she had surprised her mother by suddenly getting up and going out again. It was never proved whether the two had planned to meet again or whether their paths had crossed by chance in the dark. However, they did meet, and the encounter was to prove fateful for both Jael Denny and Thomas Drory.

Drory had clearly been contemplating murder and was carrying a strong rope in his pocket, lending weight to the view that he had coldly planned the whole act with the intention of faking a suicide. He met Jael at a stile into one of the fields and, cloaked by darkness, was able to slip a noose around her neck. Using the noose, he then threw her to the ground, causing her cloak to be torn and crushing her bonnet. He then pinned Jael down by kneeling on her chest but the girl fought back; a conclusive piece of evidence at the trial was that the dead girl was found with bite marks on her hand – marks that matched the pattern of Drory's teeth. The struggle must have been fierce.

Somehow Drory turned the struggling girl over, perhaps after a blow to the side of the head had dazed her. Then he pressed her face so hard into the ground that her nose was virtually flattened. He twisted the rope three times round her neck, strangling her,

HORRID MURDER,

Committed by a young Man on a young Woman.

George Caddell became acquainted with Miss Price and a degree of intimacy subsisted between them, and Miss Price, degraded as she was by the unfortunate step she had taken, still thought herself an equal match for one of Mr. Caddell's rank of life. As pregnancy was shortly the result of their intimacy, she repeatedly urged him to marry her, but he resisted her importunities for a considerable time. At length she heard of his paying his addresses to Miss Dean, and threatened, in case of his non-compliance, to put an end to all his prospects with that young lady, by discovering everything that had passed between them. Hereupon he formed a horrid resolution of murdering her, for he could neither bear the thought of forfeiting the esteem of a woman who he loved, nor of marrying one who had been as condescending to another as to himself. So he called on Miss Price on a Saturday and requesting her to walk with him in the fields on the following day, in order to arrange a plan for their intended marriage. Miss Price met him at the time appointed, on the road leading to Burton, at a house known by the name of "The Nag's Head." Having accompanied her supposed lover into the fields, and walked about till towards evening, they sat down under a hedge, where, after a little conversation, Caddell suddenly pulled out a knife and cut her throat, and made his escape, but not before he had waited till she was dead. In the distraction of his mind he left behind him the knife with which he had perpetrated the deed, and his case of instruments. On the following morning, Miss Price being found murdered in the field, great numbers went to take a view of the body, among whom was the woman of the house where she lodged, who recollected that she said she was going to walk with Mr. Caddell, on which the instruments were examined and sworn to have belonged to him. He was accordingly taken into custody.

J. Catnach, Printer, Monmouth Court.

Broadsheets like this by James Catnach were produced for many Victorian murders, often using the same wood block illustration, regardless that it did not quite fit the details of the crime.

then left its loose end in her hand as part of a pathetic attempt to fake suicide. An unproven rumour alleged that Drory returned to the spot two hours later and, finding Jael still alive, had finished her off by tightening the rope.

Jael's body was found early the next morning, face down under the spreading branches of a tree. Injuries to her face were so bad that 'blood was bubbling from her mouth and nose' as she was turned over. Her body was carried away on a gate. The tree later had its bark stripped off by souvenir hunters.

Drory was arrested almost immediately, his relationship with the girl being common knowledge in the district. He defended himself by saying, 'I have a letter to show it is not my child', thereby revealing that he believed the pregnancy to be the reason for the murder. But the evidence against Drory was damning, and he was tried at the same Chelmsford Assize as Sarah Chesham. In March 1851, Drory heard the sentence of death read out:

> 'The prisoner heard his fate unmoved, but before his removal from the dock he appeared to awaken to a sense of his awful situation, and was with difficulty kept from fainting.'

Whilst in prison awaiting execution, Drory openly confessed to the murder; he lay in his cell, 'for a long period groaning in the deepest distress and agony.' Given time to reflect, Drory responded to the cares of the chaplain and opened his heart to the Christian faith. On his last Sunday he went to two chapel services.

Drory's execution on 25th March 1851 attracted record crowds; Sarah Chesham was to be executed at the same time, but it was really Drory that the mostly-female crowd gathered to see. Some estimates put the crowd at over 10,000 people, including a number from Drory's home village of Doddinghurst. As the anxious crowd pressed together for a good view, thieves went to work. Spectators lost three silver watches and a gold watch as pickpockets took advantage of all the jostling. A gang of 'smashers' or forgers took the opportunity to pass counterfeit coin in the town. Badly reproduced prints of 'the execution' were sold as souvenirs. Then, unusually, the two criminals were brought to the scaffold amidst the silence of the crowd – these occasions tended to be noisy and drunken affairs. In contrast to Chesham, Drory walked forward quietly and then Hangman Calcraft covered his head with the sack. He died quickly: '. . . the next instant the drop fell. With persisted, she consented to walk there. Nature, however, and the terrors of a violent and disgraceful death were too strong for her, and she required the assistance of two persons as she moved forward. Drory appeared first on the fatal platform, and as soon as he presented himself, with drooping head and pinioned arms and faint and trembling limbs, the vast crowd of spectators assembled below were hushed into solemn and affecting silence. To the number of 6,000 or 7,000 they had been slowly gathering there from 6 o'clock in the morning ; their behaviour throughout very orderly and sedate. though the shrill voices of boys at play and the calls of orange venders might be heard at intervals. From all parts of the surrounding country the assemblage had come, it consisted principally of smockfrocked labourers, their highlows and gaiters spattered with mud, and their steps heavy with the number of miles they had travelled to "the hanging." A few farmers were present, eyeing askance the dismal implement above the gaol gateway, and thinking the minutes hours until the condemned made their appearance. There were hardly any respectable people observable in the crowd, but a most disgusting number of women. Some of these had gay flowers in their bonnets, and evidently set up for rustic belles ; others were mothers, giving suck to infants, whom they carried in their arms ; others were elderly matrons. presiding at the head of their families, and from the elevation of the domestic spring cart pointing out to their young daughters how they could best see the execution. With these exceptions, the great assemblage in front of the gaol behaved itself with much propriety. Not more than half a dozen police were visible, though Captain M'Hardy had prudently a large body in reserve. The gaol and the chief police station stand opposite each other, with a wide roadway and a piece of open ground intervening, and it was here that the spectators were chiefly assembled. Drory, when placed on the drop, was delivered over to the hands of Calcraft the executioner—who quickly drew on the white cap and adjusted the rope, while the miserable wretch ejaculated in broken accents, "This is a faithful saying, and worthy of all acceptation, that Christ Jesus came into the world to save sinners—of whom I am the chief—of whom I am the chief"—and he still kept repeating that last significant acknowledgment until the drop fell. After a delay of several minutes, during which many began to fear that there was something wrong, Sarah Chesham was with difficulty placed under the fatal beam, supported, like the other prisoner, by two attendants. Without an instant's delay Calcraft completed his simple but dreadful preparations ; and then, while with 'bated breath the thousands of spectators below looked on, the bolt was drawn ; a faint murmur of horror spread among the crowd as they saw the sentence of the law carried into effect, which was prolonged as the convulsive struggles of the dying man and woman were painfully visible. In Drory all sign of animation was extinct in four or five minutes, but Chesham struggled for six or seven. They were both light figures, and they " died hard." The crowd almost immediately after dispersed, and few remained to witness " the cutting down." As they began to separate, hawkers of ballads and " true and correct accounts" of the execution, and all kinds of edibles, appeared among them, and the assemblage was a sort of moving fair on its way back to town. The long pent-up excitement relaxed itself, much, it is to be supposed, in the same manner as the spectators of a

A contemporary press account of the double execution of Thomas Drory and Sarah Chesham.

Drory there appeared but one convulsive shake of the frame before he ceased to exist . . .' The tragic young man's body was buried within the walls of Chelmsford Gaol.

5. Tollesbury, 1851 - An Unsolved Murder?

The murder of a dredgerman's wife at a remote waterside community near Tollesbury in November 1851 proved to be one of the major 'unsolved' crimes of Victorian Essex. This was despite the fact that a large number of people were certain who the murderer was, so it is again possible that the unsatisfactory outcome of the investigation was due to the reluctance of a jury to convict on a capital offence when a shadow of doubt remained.

Elizabeth Cobb was the 33 year old wife of a Tollesbury dredgerman. They had a 7 year old child and lived in a small community of waterside houses; the child was an adopted daughter. One day at the end of November 1851, Cobb went out to work at about six in the morning, taking the family's lodger with him. He left his wife and their adopted daughter sleeping upstairs. It was the last time he saw her alive.

Just over two hours later the landlady who lived in the house opposite, Mary Wash, was alerted by the sound of the little girl screaming in the Cobb house. As the screaming did not stop she went over to investigate and uncovered the scene of a grisly murder. She found Mrs Cobb upstairs, dead in bed with frightful wounds; she was wearing only her nightdress and had been battered about the head with a heavy instrument as well as having a gashed throat. It was obvious to Mrs Wash that the house had been plundered, and it later transpired that twelve shillings had been stolen. When the doctor arrived he pronounced that Elizabeth Cobb had died of a fractured skull.

Suspicion immediately focused on Mr Cobb, but the evidence of the family lodger and his colleagues at work cleared him of any blame. However, it was not long before a sensational discovery was made – a wanderer on the path from Tollesbury to Salcott noticed a bloodstained handkerchief and stopped to investigate; he found that it was wrapped around a case containing a razor which belonged to Mrs Wash's husband!

This discovery led the investigation to the Wash household in which there were several lodgers. One of these was Mrs Wash's 20 year old brother, Harrington. He was a rather unusual character, being only five feet tall and 'of a rather forbidding expression of countenance.' The local Constable began to investigate Harrington's movements and found a lot of evidence against him. The razor, which had definitely been used on Mrs Cobb, had vanished from the house in the previous few days. A small iron ship hammer was found at the Wash house which matched the wounds on Mrs Cobb's head. So there was no doubt about how she died.

But one question remained: was it Harrington who had wielded the weapons? On the day of the murder Harrington had walked to Wivenhoe, and so it was alleged that he could have disposed of the handkerchief and razor on the way. A Wivenhoe publican claimed that Harrington had been into his pub and changed several half-crowns, yet Harrington alleged that he had only had three shillings on him. Further evidence against Harrington was found when the Constable investigated his clothes, for spots of blood were found on his trousers that the man had tried to cover up with ink. Harrington alleged that the blood came from a pig.

Though there seemed to be a lot of circumstantial evidence against Harrington, there was no definite proof. Even the presence of the hammer was not conclusive, for it was the sort of tool that many of the watermen possessed. It took the Coroner's Court three days to reach a verdict of 'Murder', an unusually long time, after which Harrington was sent for trial at the Lent Assizes of 1852.

In his trial a lot of time was given to the question of Harrington's trip to Wivenhoe and his money dealings there. Also much discussed was the question of the bloodstains on his trousers; forensic science today would have quickly cleared up whether the blood came from a human or a pig, but no such proof was available to the Victorians. In the end the jury returned a verdict of 'Not Guilty', largely because there was no definite proof that Harrington was the murderer. He walked from the court a free man.

6. Domestic Turmoil

The year of 1870 was marked by two unfortunate incidents that further emphasised the pattern of murder by persons related to the victim. Both of these incidents involved the murder of a wife by a husband and were further exacerbated by circumstances of mental illness.

The first incident occurred at Brentwood in March 1870 and involved a soldier of the Ninth Regiment. The man was based at Warley Barracks, which allowed him to be conveniently close to his wife who was able to set up home in Brentwood. However, shortly before the murder the man was sent on a tour of duty at the Isle of Grain, a remote spot in Kent where a fort guarded the Thames estuary. When the soldier came home to Brentwood he found that his wife was not at home. He must have had some suspicion about her habits, for he was able to trace her to a beerhouse where she was drinking with several soldiers. Comments were exchanged since the soldiers could not resist the chance to taunt the cuckolded husband, who threatened to fight one of them. The couple went home together, however, and all appeared to be well for the next few days.

The soldier must have been seething with barely controlled passion, for he eventually launched a furious assault on his wife whilst in the bedroom of the house, cutting her throat. Badly wounded, the woman was still able to rush out into the street and cry for help, but the furious husband simply dragged her back into the house and cut her throat again. Having murdered his wife, the deranged soldier then stood over her and cut his own throat. The incident was apparently witnessed by several men who were standing about in the street, but not a single one attempted to interfere!

The murder of Martha Finch by her husband Isaac at Sandon on 26th May 1870 was even sadder, being a typical example of how tragedy could have been averted by taking simple precautions about the mentally ill. The case was brought to light when the Finches' little girl awoke one morning to find that her mother was dead in bed and her father had gone. A neighbour, Mrs Crow, was called, who discovered that Martha Finch had been killed by five cuts and blows to the face and neck. The murder weapon was an ordinary household chopper, and this was soon found in the cook-house.

A hue and cry was set up for Isaac Finch and it wasn't long before the poor man was discovered hiding in a nearby ditch. He was promptly arrested. At his trial in July 1870 some sad details about the case emerged. The daughter said that her father had been 'in low spirits' in recent weeks whilst Mrs Crow said that Martha had confided in her that she was frightened about Isaac; he had apparently scared her by turning up his eyes. Further information was produced about Isaac Finch's background; he had been in a mental asylum for some time, but had got married after being released and had seemed quite happy with life. However, there must have been a family condition as two of Finch's uncles had died in asylums and another was in one at the time of his trial.

Under these sad circumstances there could be little doubt about the verdict and Finch was found 'Not Guilty' of Wilful Murder on the grounds of his insanity. He was taken to Broadmoor.

7. The Purfleet Child Murder, 1874

In the second half of Victoria's reign executions ceased to be practised in public. This was largely as a result of the frightful behaviour at public executions, when drunken and debauched behaviour was commonplace. The matter attracted the attention of Parliament, and from the start of 1867 executions were conducted within the prison walls. The first Essex execution to be conducted in private was that of Michael Campbell, who was executed on 24th April 1871 for the murder of Samuel Galloway at Stratford. There was then a gap of several years until 29th March 1875, when Richard Coate was executed for a particularly nasty murder at Purfleet in December 1874.

Richard Coate was a 22 year old sergeant in the Royal Artillery and was based at Purfleet, where he taught in the school. On of his pupils was little Alice Boughen, aged 6, who was last seen alive at 3pm on 9th December. She was the child of the commandant's servant, and when the girl did not return home after school a search was begun. It ended at 6am the next morning when little Alice's body was found in the marshes 40 yards from her school.

The condition of the child's body horrified the district and the local press. One newspaper reported that 'The appearance of the body led to the conclusion that a murder had been committed, after an outrage of an horrible nature had been attempted.'

Several people had already commented that the schoolmaster's behaviour the previous evening had been rather odd. He had been seen in the barracks canteen on the evening of Alice's disappearance in an agitated and trembling state, with his clothes in a mess. He had then gone back to the barracks, saying that he felt ill, and had gone to bed at an unusually early time. Investigations were started immediately and it was found that Coate's shirt, jacket,

Chelmsford gaol where Richard Coate was executed in 1874 for the murder of a six year old girl at Purfleet.

trousers and bed linen were all covered with blood. Hair found on the clothes matched that of Alice, who by this time was known to have died of a fractured skull. There couldn't be any doubt that she was murdered, and Coate could offer no satisfactory explanation for the state of his clothes. There had also been reports of a loud cry from the school toilet having been heard at about 3.20pm on the day Alice died.

Coate eventually confessed fully to what he had done. He admitted that on the afternoon of the murder the child had been sitting on his knee, playing, but had then asked to go outside. He had assaulted the girl in the closet and killed her there, but had then taken the body outside with the intention of throwing it into the River Thames. For some reason he never did this but went off to the barracks, leaving the remainder of his pupils unattended.

Richard Coate was tried at Chelmsford in March 1875 but the trial was largely a formality and he was duly found to be guilty. He wore his uniform throughout the trial, but on return to the prison afterwards it was stripped off him. Whilst awaiting execution Coate used the same cells as had been occupied by another murderer, Karl Kohl, a German who had committed murder on Plaistow Marshes years before.

Coate was the first person to be hanged at Chelmsford by a new executioner, Marwood. His predecessor, Calcraft, had used a drop of three feet but Marwood increased this to five feet to speed the victim's death. Richard Coate was praying for forgiveness when he died.

8. Leigh, 1886: An Extraordinary Death

The distinction between Wilful Murder and Manslaughter was a crucial one that sometimes led to complex legal arguments, but it was fortunate that the legal authorities for once had a clear-headed view about an extraordinary death that occurred at Leigh in January 1886.

The incident involved the Murrell family, who lived at Ferguson's Cottages at the foot of Leigh Hill. The father was a waterman and he had two young sons of 13 and 11 years. One day a visiting aunt decided to be generous (doubtless she later wished she had not been) and gave the two boys two large shut-knives and sixpence each.

When their parents were out the two boys began playing together. William, the eldest, got annoyed with his brother Frederick and shut him in a cupboard to the distress of the younger boy. When Freddie was released he was in such a fury that he stuck his knife into William. William limped round to a neighbour's house for help, saying, 'My brother has stuck me with a knife'. The boy was wounded in the thigh and losing blood, so the neighbour bound a towel round the gash and sent for the doctor. But the doctor was unable to stop the loss of blood. William became unconscious and died at 8 o'clock that evening.

Frederick was taken to Southend Police station and, at the age of eleven, Frederick Murrell was charged with Wilful Murder. Frederick openly confessed that he had done it, telling the Police Constable: 'He would not let me alone. He fastened me in a cupboard, and when I got out I stuck the knife in him. I did not intend to hurt him.'

Rumours of insanity in the family began to circulate, though there was nothing to suggest that Freddie had suffered anything worse than a fit of bad temper. A cousin of his had been involved in a stabbing incident at the *Billet Inn* five years previously, while it was alleged that another relative had committed suicide in a water butt.

The Coroner very sensibly decided that this was not a case of Wilful Murder as it was not premeditated and the boy had not intended to actually kill his brother. Frederick was sent forward to the next Assize on a charge of Manslaughter, where the case was very sensibly dismissed.

9. Some Other Murders and Attempted Murders

In an age when access to contraception was rare, the crime of child murder was quite common. Related to it was the crime of 'concealing a birth'. Many unfortunate girls became pregnant in difficult circumstances, and their attempts to give birth to the child without detection sometimes resulted in the death of the baby.

In January 1847 a seven week old child died suddenly at Dunmow and the local surgeon, Thomas Bell, concluded that the child had been affected by convulsions. The mother, Sarah Bright, was unmarried and people soon began to allege that she had murdered the child with a dose of opium that she had obtained in Chelmsford. At the time the opium, from which heroin is derived, was freely used as a drug to quieten children.

At the Lent Assizes of March 1867 a servant girl, Emma Davis from Manuden, appeared on a charge of having murdered her baby on 23rd January. The situation for servants was particularly difficult as marriage would involve losing their job, but so would an illegitimate pregnancy. Emma Davis successfully concealed the fact that she was pregnant at all for several months, but on the day in question she had to stop her housework and go to bed soon after noon. At 3.30pm she told a fellow servant that she was all right and would come down again later, but at 5.15pm two short cries were heard in her room. Her colleague was alerted by this, but Emma told her that she had had a miscarriage. She said she had put the baby under her bed for a while and then disposed of it down the closet.

The circumstances were sufficient to arouse doubts in the other servant's mind, and the closet was investigated. A baby was found in it, lying face down on the bricks at the bottom and quite dead. Its body was hauled out and it was found that the child had been killed by a tape twisted round its neck. At a trial a surgeon gave details of how the child had died, during which Emma Davis fainted. She was punished with eighteen months hard labour.

Child murder was not always an easy crime to prove as it was relatively common and in larger towns the bodies of babies turned up occasionally with no real proof as to their identity. Eliza Cheverton, for example, a 28 year old widow from Colchester was accused of murdering her daughter Emma in July 1861 by drowning her in the river. She was found to be 'Not Guilty' because of a lack of proof about how the event happened.

Sometimes women were forced into rash acts through the desperation of their circumstances. In an age when there was no unemployment or family benefit, large numbers of children were difficult to feed and most families had a rightful dread of going to the workhouse. In January 1850 Milicent Page appeared at her sister's house in the middle of the night, bleeding profusely from a wound in the throat. Her sister went back with Milicent to her home and found her baby there, also bleeding from a neck wound but wrapped up in bedclothes. An open razor was nearby. It transpired that Page had decided to do away with her baby in a fit of depression as her husband's wages had recently been reduced; having attacked the baby she had then attempted to kill herself too. She told her sister that the baby was 'a great trouble' to her.

At her first trial, Mrs Page burst into tears so frequently that the judge decided to remand her whilst an investigation was made into her sanity. When she reappeared in court it was felt that her problems could best be solved by keeping her in safe custody as she seemed to be a danger to herself and others.

Drink played a part in a number of violent assaults, as detailed in several chapters of this book. Sometimes drunken brawls led to death as with a case at Great Dunmow in 1862. Henry Eagle, 'a powerful-looking man', was accused of killing James Barnard, an umbrella hawker. Both parties to the incident had spent most of the evening in a public house and met up after a few too many drinks. They got into an argument about their relative experiences in the army. Eagle tripped Barnard up, but the hawker replied by hitting his assailant over the head with an umbrella. Eagle then hit Barnard in the stomach; the latter decided that this was quite enough, and set off to summon Police help. Eagle followed Barnard to a spot near the pond, where he attacked him from behind with a six inch blade. Barnard was stabbed in the abdomen and back-bone, dying from his wounds. As with most drunken brawls, a verdict of Manslaughter was returned, for which Eagle received ten years penal servitude.

Insanity, whether induced by drink or not, was frequently discussed in the courts. In 1847 James Willsmore of Rochford murdered John Terry. Willsmore was described as 'of a very youthful and simple appearance' and was aged about 17. He attacked Terry, who was an old man, on the highway with the intention of robbing him. The old man received a severe mouth wound, from which he bled badly, but Willsmore ran off and left him dying at the scene of the assault. Willsmore was formally sentenced to death, but the jury entered a plea for mercy on account of him being mentally defective and the case was referred to the Queen.

In March 1848 Martha Prior was tried for the murder of her baby at Great Waltham. The defence produced a case that stressed the insanity of the woman and so the jury recorded a verdict of 'Not Guilty on the grounds of insanity.' Such verdicts appear to have been more common in Victorian times than they are now.

Bungled murder attempts were quite common; it was rare for an Assize to pass without a trial for attempted murder or some grievous form of assault. Typical was George Gunn of Tilty, who fittingly used a shotgun in an effort to murder his sister after a family row. Ann Gunn managed to grab hold of the gun causing her brother to miss his shot; the weapon fired harmlessly into the fireplace, then the other sisters in the family came to the rescue.

A more sensational case of attempted murder came to light in 1899 when Elizabeth Walford of Halstead was put on trial. She was a 19 year old servant girl and was accused of having tried to poison her mistress, Elizabeth Marlar, with 'strychnia' in December 1898. The source of the dispute was a common one — Mrs Marlar had put a stop to a correspondence between her servant girl and a young man named Rayner. No doubt the girl therefore had good reason to feel upset, so it was rather strange that shortly afterwards she brought Mrs Marlar tea and toast while the mistress of the house was still in her room. This was a departure from the usual routine. The following day the girl brought tea and toast to Mrs Marlar's room again, but this time the woman noticed that the toast tasted bitter.

Her suspicions aroused, Mrs Marlar sent the offending toast to the local chemist for analysis, and he reported that it contained strychnia; this was commonly used as rat poison. When Mr Marlar intervened and questioned Elizabeth Walford, the girl broke down and attempted suicide. She was brought to court and given eight months hard labour. It was a sad case, but one that perfectly reflects the reality of 'upstairs' and 'downstairs' relationships at a time when domestic servants could be the virtual slaves of their employers.

THIEVES AT LARGE

I T is a sad fact that for many years crimes against property, like theft or arson, were more severely punished than crimes of violence against the person. When Queen Victoria ascended the throne it was only a very few years since Essex had witnessed the execution of persons for theft and in 1829 a boy from Witham had been executed for arson. For much of the Victorian era thieves continued to be punished by transportation, a sentence which was quite likely to result in the death of the prisoner in any case. Yet some quite violent assaults were punished with small fines.

Crimes against property seem to have terrified the Victorian upper classes greatly. The noted social historian, Derek Fraser, has written that 'most nineteenth century crime was concerned with gain', and certainly a lot of it does appear to have been. Perhaps the reason for this was that an enormous number of people lived on or below the breadline; the starving could turn to the Poor Law for help, but many feared the harsh environment of the workhouse where all freedom was lost. A number of people would therefore turn to petty crime in order to feed their families during difficult times, especially as there was no social security payment to help through unemployment. It is also possible that sheer fury at the conspicuously unequal distribution of wealth spurred some people into crime, though this is likely to have been less important than the fact that the small-time criminal had a good chance of getting away with it.

1. A Catalogue of Thieves

A lot of crimes that were punished severely seem minor to us. In January 1839 William Kitchen, a 14 year old from Coggeshall, was arrested for stealing a loaf of bread from a shop. He was described as a 'hardened urchin' who had been in trouble several times before. Because of this he was given a sentence of ten years transportation to Australia, which seems a very severe punishment for stealing a loaf of bread! The reporter described the boy's reaction to this news: 'The sentence appeared to have very little effect on him, and we understand he actually threatened to have his revenge on one of the witnesses, whenever he regained his liberty.' Before sending him abroad, it was decided to place him in the 'General Penitentiary' to see if his character could be changed.

A common type of theft was the stealing of farm produce, particularly straw and grain. Thomas Hymas was clearly a hardened character in this area, as he was given seven years transportation in 1839 for stealing twenty-five bushels of wheat. On his return to Essex he settled around the Dunton area, and in March 1847 stole a truss of clover hay. So he ended up back in court, this time being given fifteen years transportation. Hymas was a straw carter by trade, and clearly could not resist the temptation of pilfering his load. In 1866 a waggoner was taking a load of hay from Great Dunmow to London, and was near the village of Fyfield when he noticed that some of his load was missing. He saw Henry Hull with another cart, in which the man was attempting to cover something over with a coat. Police investigation revealed that Hull had stolen 27lbs of hay; by this time sentences had been eased, and Hull received only nine months hard labour.

Another hay thief, George Murrells of Vange, was caught through some simple detective work. In December 1881 a farm bailiff at Vange issued orders to some men to cut down some hay and cart it to the Hall Farm. When the bailiff went back to the stack yard later on, his attention was caught by a pile of straw in which he found that two trusses had been hidden. It was clear to him that one of the men planned to take a share in the work! The bailiff contacted Constable Brown, and the two men spied on the stack yard until 11 o'clock that night but without success. As it was the middle of winter they gave up their watch, but put two pieces of paper (on which they had written) into the middle of the trusses. When they returned the next morning the two trusses had gone, but they were able to follow the traces of dropped hay to George Murrell's cottage a quarter of a mile away. Four trusses of hay were found in his yard, two of which contained the fatal pieces of paper. Murrells had committed a similar crime 30 years before and that time was given 3 years in prison; on this occasion he escaped with 3 months hard labour.

Attacks on the highway were also quite common. The age of the 'highwayman' had passed, but the 'footpad' still flourished – these were criminals who waylaid pedestrians in much the same way as the mugger does today.

Typical of the 'footpad' style of crime, which could occur in the town or the country, was an attack on Italian Sabino Piazintine at Ingatestone in October 1866. Piazintine had come to England to sell religious images, and he was carrying a basket of them and 25 shillings when attacked. Two young men, James Rutland and Henry Guy, stopped him and wrenched the basket away from his grasp. Finding nothing of interest in it, they dropped it on the road. Guy, who was wearing a 'Scotch cap', attacked the Italian with what was called a 'life preserver'; this type of weapon could vary, but was usually a strip of canvas filled with sand or lead. It could be hidden up the sleeve, and then wielded to savage effect. A screwdriver was also used in the attack, and left behind – bloodied – on the road. Piazintine was severly beaten and robbed, but was probably saved from worse harm by the appearance of two other travellers who chased the criminals off. Rutland was found hiding in a ditch with the life preserver nearby and Guy was soon trapped as well. At the trial Piazintine had to speak through an interpreter. Both men were given eighteen months hard labour whilst Guy received an additional twenty lashes of the cat o' nine tails.

This type of violence was common for the footpad, but the use of firearms was unusual. In 1847 a carter going from London to Ongar was stopped between Fyfield and Beauchamp Roding by two men armed with pistols. They stole £5 and two knives from the man. A chase was started, with the two thieves being traced towards Romford, but the trail went cold at Stapleford Abbott.

The drivers of waggons were prone to attack, because they were likely to be carrying goods of value but could only move slowly and thus could easily be surprised by a pedestrian. Jane Vandervord was the 'carrier' between Gravesend and Horndon in 1847, which means that she operated a rather slow form of general goods transport. In April that year she was passing through Mucking when a youth, George Wood, began to follow her. He followed for three miles, obviously choosing his spot carefully,

An Essex country lane between Braintree and the Notleys. The narrow roads with dense hedges offered many opportunities for footpads to waylay travellers and farmers returning from market with money in their pockets.

then he attacked her with an ash stick. She was struck on the head and Wood threatened to kill her unless she handed over the money. It was a classic 'Money or your life!' situation, but Jane Vandervord only had sixpence on her! When Wood was arrested he was in serious trouble, because Highway Robbery and Wounding was still a capital offence. However, the woman's injuries were not serious and so he was given 15 years transportation.

One of the problems of catching footpads and similar criminals was producing the evidence to prove that a certain individual was responsible. James Dixey, a youth of about 19 years, was accused of a highway robbery at Mark's Tey in December 1850, but when brought to trial the following month was discharged through lack of evidence. It was alleged that Dixey, a labourer, had attacked Robert Chaplin of Mark's Tey Hall at about 8.30pm on a winter night. There seemed to be plenty of evidence against Dixey before the case reached court, but somehow it all evaporated as soon as the trial commenced. Dixey had been seen hiding in the hedge earlier that evening, but there were allegations that the witness to this 'had been tampered with'. Dixey's little brother William had earlier not been able to offer any support to his brother's alibi, but in court the boy declared that James Dixey had been in bed at 8pm on the evening in question. The rest of Dixey's family all swore the same thing, and so he escaped without punishment.

Most of these 'muggings' were the result of spontaneous reaction to an opportunity rather than careful pre-planning. In January 1852 James Squires was walking to Warley when he was stopped by two Privates who were in the service of the East India Company. One of the soldiers knocked him down, then they held him on the ground whilst his neckerchief was twisted round his throat to keep him quiet. The soldiers rifled Squires' pockets and stole 2s. 6d. When they let him go he followed them at a safe distance and saw them go into Warley Barracks. One of the soldiers foolishly boasted to a friend that he'd given a navvy a good kicking along the road, was overheard by a corporal, and he was arrested.

It was much safer to be a footpad if you operated in a pair, since one man could disable the victim whilst the other searched his pockets. Some footpads even used a female accomplice to lure the victim into a secluded place. George Joslin of Moreton was attacked near Ongar in November 1885 by two men, one of whom held him in a ditch whilst the other stole £1-3-6d. The two thieves were later caught though, and given 12 months and 8 months hard labour respectively.

The fruits of this sort of crime were often only small. A prize victim was an unwary farmer coming back from market with money in his pocket and too much alcohol in his head, but sensible travellers always travelled with company. A serious incident took place between Saffron Walden and Ashdon in December 1898, involving an elderly gardener named Thomas Hurst. Hurst had recently moved to Ashdon, and a few days before Christmas walked into Saffron Walden to deposit his lifetime's savings of £130 in the Post Office Savings Bank. Most of this he took in the form of gold, but at the Post Office was told that no-one could deposit more than £50 in one year without special arrangements. To deposit his money, Hurst would have had to sign some documents but he had paralysis in one hand and so could not sign; he went out again, still with all the money. Foolishly he then visited two or three of the town's pubs, including the *Royal Oak* where he fell into rough company. He started talking to two men who were sceptical about how far he could walk as he was such an old man. Hurst challenged them to a bet, but when he put a sovereign on the table it promptly disappeared – a trick that a man of his age should have been aware of! The two men then tried to rob his pockets, so Hurst decided that it was time to leave. Percy Scotcher, one of the troublemakers, decided that he would accompany Hurst back to Ashdon – much against Hurst's will. Scotcher waited until they reached a lonely spot along the road, then assaulted the old man and stole his money. Hurst was later found moaning on the road by a Constable; Scotcher was easily apprehended and taken to the Assizes, from where he was despatched to prison.

Sometimes people were punished for very minor crimes. To take one week in January 1862 as an example, a number of petty offences emerge. David Ratford, aged 16, stole a piece of apple pudding and a slice of bread from a Layer bailiff. The boy lived in the same house as the bailiff and simply took the food from the pantry; he was given seven days hard labour. William Rose was only 10, but he stole a rabbit from the yard of the *Falcon Inn* at Wivenhoe, for which he received 10 days hard labour. Charles Kelly, a servant, stole a garden fork from his master at Great Baddow; dishonesty amongst servants was regarded as very serious, and Kelly got 6 weeks hard labour.

These sentences seem quite light in comparison to what happened to Jonah Beckwith of Bocking. He stole some potatoes from his neighbours and was given five years penal servitude!

Pubs were an ideal hunting ground for the thief. In Braintree in 1863 Joseph Clark of Felsted was drinking at the *Green Man* when, in typical fashion, he was lured into the back room of the pub by a female who offered him certain services. Whilst his attention was so diverted, two men were able to follow him into the room and relieve him of 1½ sovereigns. Clark did not discover the loss until the landlord asked him to pay the bill, but the landlord immediately realised who was responsible for the crime and the two men were arrested.

Another case that involved a prostitute was at Harwich in 1872. One man who learnt his lesson in the most public way possible was John Brander, who held the Army rank of Captain. He spent a very drunken evening in the less salubrious part of Harwich, ending up in the company of Elizabeth Gardener who was a prostitute. The next morning Brander discovered that he had lost forty guineas – a foolishly large sum of money to carry around on a drunken spree. Gardener was arrested, but claimed in court that the Captain had given the money to her. The Captain himself, perhaps conveniently, claimed that he couldn't remember any of that evening's events. Gardener agreed to hand the money back to the foolish soldier, and was then released.

A fairly unusual type of theft was committed by William Green, a postman from Belchamp St. Paul's. Green was a regular visitor to the ale-house and had got himself into difficulty, so the trust involved in delivering the mails became too great for him. He stole £2 from a letter that a servant girl was sending to her widowed mother. At the trial great play was made upon the plight of the ailing mother, and also about how the postal service could not operate if postmen behaved like Green. He was punished severely, with 14 years transportation.

During the winter of 1874 John Cooper was ploughing at Feering when he discovered that his coat, which he had taken off, had vanished. Cooper hurried to Mark's Tey to inform Sergeant Buck, and a rumour spread that a man had been seen going towards Colchester wearing Cooper's coat. The Sergeant gave chase and caught the man at Stanway. He questioned the man as to his name and address, both of which the thief denied knowing. This pretence of stupidity failed to rescue him from being taken into custody.

2. Animal Stealing

The theft of animals was not an activity confined to the cattle rustlers of the American West, but was in fact widely practised in Victorian Essex. Most famous amongst this type of crime was poaching, but farm animals were also stolen on a small and large scale. The most common type of animal to be stolen was the sheep rather than the cow; it appealed mostly to poor people in search of a rare taste of meat, as a sheep could be easily killed and skinned under cover of darkness. The meat could then be cut up and hidden relatively easily, but a cow was altogether a different proposition.

In the early part of the Victorian era the theft of farm animals was regarded as particularly serious. A lot of it was done on a small scale by casual rather than habitual criminals, rather like

James Chaplin of Feering who was sentenced to 7 years transportation in 1839 for stealing a pig. A near-neighbour of his, Thomas Belcham, was a pig-dealer who bought pigs at the market at Colchester and then took them to Romford for sale. Large numbers of animals were a common sight on the road in those days. On 1st December 1838 Belcham bought 87 pigs at Colchester, presumably with an eye to the Christmas trade, and took them back to Feering. The next morning Belcham's son found that there was one pig missing. Investigation soon showed that the gate had been undone in the night, and from there tracks led to Chaplin's cottage. At the cottage Belcham found his pig in Chaplin's rabbit pen, though Chaplin claimed he had found it wandering in the road. The case was proved when Belcham discovered a sow at Chaplin's as well, which he had lost two months before. The wonder is that Chaplin made so little attempt to hide the animals; most animal thieves killed their prizes as soon as possible.

An idealised Victorian view of country life for the poor — a warm family home with grace being said before a big satisfying meal. The reality was very different. Many men were driven to sheep stealing to feed their starving families.

Chaplin was very small-scale compared to the organised criminals of the Hatfield Broad Oak and Debden Gangs who were operating in 1838,–9. The Debden Gang was a group of labourers aged between 17 and 24 who stole from a number of places in the district and processed the goods through the house of Mrs S. Marshall in Debden. The gang included John Haydon, David Haydon and Francis Clark. Clark was clearly the ringleader. He was a hardened criminal who had been in custody 15 times between 1827 and 1839. The gang was responsible for a huge number of crimes. As examples they stole 7 fowls at Debden in March 1838, 7 ducks from the same place in December that year, 2 pigs from Thaxted in the same month and in April 1838 they killed 2 lambs at Wimbish. The 'fence', Mrs Marshall, was also capable of theft and made a habit of stealing beans from local farmers with the assistance of her 16 year old daughter, Mary.

This sort of habitual crime was bound to be traced eventually, and after the disappearance of the Debden ducks in December 1838, Constable Stunt turned up at the Marshall house. A search revealed pillows stuffed with duck feathers. Marshall claimed that the feathers came from her own ducks which had been killed by a sow.

The whole gang ended up in court in February 1839 and were dealt a variety of punishments. Mary Marshall was let off with a warning, but her mother received six months hard labour. The men were more severely punished, each receiving transportation. John and David Haydon got 7 and 10 years respectively, whilst Clark was transported for 14 years.

The Debden gang were almost amateurs in comparison to the Hatfield Broad Oak Gang who were operating at about the same time. This gang consisted of John and James Dodd, who owned a farm of 100 acres, and their servant William Coe. The fact that they were farmers themselves made their activities all the more scandalous. In October 1838 a farmer named Buckland sent ten heifers to Eastwick in Hertfordshire for grazing, but three of the animals disappeared, even though one of these had distinctive markings on its hide and would have been a risky animal to steal.

The Dodds' farm was actually searched in connection with another crime, but several hides were found freshly buried. This alerted suspicion, as the animals would have been worth a great deal more if killed a month later. On investigation, one of the hides was found to have the distinctive markings of Buckland's missing animals. As evidence was gathered against the brothers, it was found that Coe had also stolen twenty lambs from the nearby farm of a Mr Bentall, which the brothers had then 'processed'. No doubt because of their position in society, the Hatfield Broad Oak Gang received severe punishment – James Dodd was transported for life, William Coe for 30 years, and John Dodd for 29 years.

The most common type of animal stealing was the killing and skinning of a sheep at night, usually done to feed the criminal's family rather than for profit. John Nichols, a weaver from Great Coggeshall, committed exactly this sort of crime in February 1866. The sheep concerned came from the flock of W.G. Dennis, who farmed Monk Downs, and all his sheep were distinctively marked. One morning Dennis' son noticed that one animal was missing from the flock. A search soon brought to light the skin of a sheep, which had been tied up with a piece of waste cord – commonly used in the silk trade – and dumped in a ditch about a quarter of a mile from Nichols' home.

On the night in question Nichols had been seen out near the sheep field, but had claimed that he was going fishing. The silk cord seemed an important link, as Nichols worked in silk weaving, and Sergeant Bacon went to his house. A search revealed a number of small pieces of mutton around the house, including some that was resting innocently on the table. When questioned, Nichols claimed that he had found the mutton in the park.

Despite expert evidence from Sergeant Bacon, who had once been a butcher, Nichols was acquitted. The jury maintained, to the displeasure of the judge, that having mutton was no evidence of having stolen it. It was a typical case.

3. Burglary

Burglary, which was a quite specific offence involving the breaking into a house, was regarded as very serious too, though expert burglars appear to have been fairly rare in Victorian Essex. Early in 1839 it was reported that Braintree was being 'terrorised' by a gang of burglars, but this seems to have been a typical exaggeration by a reporter. A gang of four men was soon brought before the magistrates (if their offences were serious they would have gone to the next Assize) and given minor punishments. One of the men was clearly something of a cheeky character, as he appeared before the Bench wearing a neckerchief which he had stolen from Thomas Rolfe!

Debden was obviously an area with a crime problem about 1839–1840, as in the latter year there was a major case of burglary involving another local gang. In October 1840, 5 young men and 3 young women were tried for burglary on the premises of John White at Debden. During a night in July, White's housekeeper had been woken by noises downstairs, and she woke her master. He went down and surprised the men who had just broken into the house through the pantry. White rushed back upstairs to charge a gun, but the intruders came running up after him and one managed to grab the gun. James Daice pointed the gun at White and demanded, 'Your money or your life.'

The burglars emptied White's pockets of 3 sovereigns and 10 half-sovereigns, then proceeded to ransack the house. They took money, cutlery, silver and even wine; White's servant had a smock stolen, which he later saw a man wearing at the Newport House of Correction!

Having taken all they wanted, the gang disappeared. White summoned the Constable, and a hunt began. The entire gang, including their 3 women, was found in a field at Great Hadham; they had consumed all the wine, and were so intoxicated that 2 were handcuffed before they woke up!

The gang was discovered to have been the same one that had committed burglary in Saffron Walden the week before, when they had also used threatening behaviour. They were all tried for both crimes in October 1840, and found guilty. The girls laughed out loud when the verdict was read out. All the men were transported for life, but the females were given only twelve months hard labour as they had not actually entered the houses.

A larger scale crime was committed at Waltham Holy Cross in 1851, when there was a carefully organised raid on the powder works there that netted the considerable sum of £450 which belonged to Her Majesty's Ordnance. The raid was organised by a local publican with the help of two men who worked in the powder works. They were all transported.

To rob your relatives seemed a particularly obnoxious crime, but when this was committed at Stansted Mountfichet in 1862 it was only lightly punished despite a large sum of money being involved. William Luck was an old bachelor and something of a miser, for he kept his life's savings of £100 in a box, but never did anything with the money. All his relatives knew about it, and for some the temptation was too powerful. Luck kept the money box hidden in the thatch of his house, but some relatives and friends knew its exact location.

One day Luck found that his money box had gone. A Police Constable was called, and he searched the house of James and Catherine Luck. The Constable found that Catherine had bought quite a lot of new clothes in the previous few days. He also discovered four new purses, each full of gold. William Brett, a family friend, was also known to have been celebrating – he had bought a supply of steak and gin, and had drunk a pint of brandy straight down, but suddenly Brett was nowhere to be found.

It emerged that Catherine Luck had stolen the money box from her relative's house with the help of Brett, who had discovered the hiding place. James Luck had burnt the box in an effort to hide the evidence. All were eventually arrested; the Lucks got 6 months hard labour and Brett got 12 months as he had absconded.

A year later there was another burglary at Stansted Mountfichet. Clement Fletcher broke into the house of William White on a Saturday night; it was too dark to find anything valuable, so he helped himself to some pie from the pantry and settled down on the sofa to wait for dawn. At 7 o'clock on the Sunday morning, a servant girl came down the stairs to find the house in chaos. Guessing what had happened, she went back to summon White down too. White came down, saw the chaos, and then noticed that the cellar door was open. He suspected that the criminal might still be in the cellar and was just about to go down into it when a man yelled out and a pistol was fired. Fletcher, who had gone to sleep on the sofa and had not been noticed, had woken up. The shot harmlessly hit the staircase, and White was able to run off for help. Fletcher tried to escape into the garden, but was trapped by the high wall that ran round the back of White's property. He was arrested at gunpoint by White and despatched to the Assizes. Truly a case of being caught napping!

North-east Essex was troubled by a burglar in late 1862. William Simpson was the culprit, and he had a particularly active Sunday afternoon at Langham once. From one house he stole a pair of child's boots, then he went to the house of the schoolmistress at Great Horkesley who was out at church. From there he stole a silver watch, four spoons and some clothes. That night he went on to Langham Hall, where he stole a rug by entering through the cookhouse.

After midnight Simpson found his way to Dedham, and his orgy of burgling continued. This time he was not so lucky; having entered the drawing room of a Mr Cobbold, he knocked something over and disturbed the owner of the house. Cobbold crept downstairs and found the burglar at work, but Simpson nimbly escaped through the window. Cobbold, who was wearing only his slippers and a dressing gown, gave chase and pursued the burglar around the garden. The gallant man managed to catch up with Simpson, wrestled him to the ground, and a struggle ensued. During this Simpson's fingers got into Cobbold's mouth, and the furious man gave Simpson a good bite. Simpson, though, was able to make his escape, though he left the stolen goods and his hat behind. Simpson was later arrested at a pub in Colchester, the conclusive evidence being the marks of Cobbold's teeth in his thumb!

There were, of course, many hundreds of thefts committed in Victorian Essex, but to conclude this chapter we can take three examples which summarise the whole business.

A typical feature was the known and habitual criminal, who committed a crime so often that it was easy to catch him. Israel Leet of Lawford, for example, was a known poacher, so when the local Constable saw him going out with his dog at 11 o'clock at night in the middle of winter, the Constable was naturally suspicious.

The Constable followed Leet and his dog into a field, where the dog drove the sheep into one corner and then seized one, ripping its throat. The dog then discovered the Constable hiding in the field, which caused Leet to make a frantic bid for freedom over a stile. The Constable, perhaps inspired by superhuman forces, managed to throw his truncheon at Leet in the dark and actually hit the fleeing criminal on the head. Leet was knocked out by this amazing blow! He received 6 months hard labour as a punishment.

The picking of pockets was another typical crime, practised whenever large crowds made it safe. The Harwich Naval Review of May 1863 attracted such large crowds that pickpockets were at work on the railway stations long before anyone actually got to Harwich. Philip Bennet was amongst the crowd waiting on

Public executions attracted vast crowds. While their attention was on the gallows they were easy prey to pick-pockets.

Witham station for a train to Harwich, when he felt a man brush against him. He looked down and found that his purse had been half-lifted out of his pocket. Bennet pursued the man who had jostled him into the station toilet and, with the aid of a porter, trapped him there. Bennet then found that he had lost his watch, which had been removed from its chain. The man trapped in the toilet, James MacDonald, was not responsible for this, but Joseph Smith was found to be the guilty man. Both Smith and MacDonald were known thieves from London, who had come out to Essex with several others of their type for the big occasion. They each received 3 months hard labour.

Saddest of all, though, were the miserable beggars who existed at the very bottom level of society. One of these was Daniel Price, described by the *Essex Standard* as a 'miserable-looking being', who had been in and out of the workhouse on numerous occasions. Price was seen acting suspiciously in the area of the Great Eastern Railway's yard at Harwich, and the Constable who had spotted him watched as Price stole 28lbs of coal from the GER's heap. For this he was given 31 days hard labour.

ROMANCE, PASSION
AND THE LACK OF IT

❧ ◇ ❧

IN Victorian times the laws governing marriage, and the various
fruits of love, were very different to the present situation. A
married woman, for example, had virtually no legal rights over
her husband or even her property until the Married Women's
Property Act of 1870 began a slow process of reform. The 1857
Matrimonial Causes Act, for example, provided for secular
means of divorce but the grounds on which the female could
petition were much more limited than the grounds for male
complaint. It was not until 1878 that another Matrimonial Causes
Act made the husband's violence against the wife grounds for
separation. Against this background, a number of spectacular legal
cases were fought out on issues such as 'Breach of Promise'. Less
attention was given to giving children legal protection against
sexual exploitation. Up until 1885 the age of consent was only 13,
but then the Criminal Law Amendment Act raised the level to 16
in an effort to combat child prostitution. The myth of 'Victorian
values' has often been written about, but it is the issues of sex and
family that most reveal the hypocrisy of many Victorians.

1. Marriage Vows
The law about marriage could be quite complex, though it is
true to say that marriage was treated very seriously as a legal
institution. An example of this was the Victorian tendency to have
'Breach of Promise' lawsuits where an individual had backed out
of a proposed marriage. Generally speaking an engagement was

considered to be legally binding, but doubt sometimes focused on whether a formal engagement had been contracted or not.

Breach of Promise cases usually received a lot of attention in the press, so they cannot have been brought lightly. Personal details of both parties could be exposed to the amusement of the reading public. An instance of this was the 1862 Breach of Promise case brought by Ann Brown against George Strutt, both being from West Mersea.

Ann Brown, the plaintiff, was a barmaid to whom Strutt had taken a fancy. He must have been a moderately wealthy character, and he asked Ann Brown to become 'manager' of his house with the prospect of marriage. Miss Brown was to be rudely awoken, however, because Strutt seduced her and ill-treated her, without ever repeating his offer of marriage. She decided to take him to court, as he had seduced her under false pretences.

Strutt must have been a bit of a character, because he appeared in the courtroom in a manner of dress intended to create the impression of extreme poverty. He was described by a reporter:

'Considerable merriment was caused by the ostensibly poverty-stricken appearance of the defendant, who presented himself in a battered wide-awake, long leather buskins well besmearched with dirt, a rough unkempt head of hair, a coat ragged and buttonless, apparently requiring an old leather strap which encircled his waist to keep it in anything like position and prevent it being blown off his back in fragments.'

This disguise clearly did Strutt no good at all, since damages were awarded against him of £200, a very hefty sum.

The normal pattern of these cases was for a relatively poor female to bring action against a more prosperous male. Often the wealthy male had secured the seduction of some gullible servant on the promise of marriage with no serious intention in that direction at all. Cases such as that could have serious implications, but other Breach of Promise cases introduced a touch of hilarity into the courtroom.

One such lighthearted case took place in Braintree in 1871. The plaintiff was a 27 year old dressmaker who lived with her uncle at the 'Boar's Head' public house in Braintree. The defendant was an old man, aged 73, who was the farmer of 40 acres. It was a typical case of an old man infatuated with a younger woman, with the

The full majesty of a Victorian courtroom.

latter hoping to reap some benefit from the situation. The farmer definitely proposed marriage and the girl accepted, but an argument arose over the old man's will. The woman said that he should provide for her in the event of his death (which seemed quite imminent), but the old man refused to change it. On these grounds she took him to court for breach of promise. When the old farmer appeared to give evidence, it was found that he had lost all his teeth and so no-one could understand what he was saying. Nonetheless the court found against him, and the dressmaker was awarded damages of a farthing. This showed that, although she was legally right, the court disapproved of her motives. They were doubtless suspicious of the 46 year age gap between the two 'lovers'.

An interfering mother was the cause of another 'Breach of

Promise' case that was at the centre of legal argument in 1898 and 1899. William Hunt was a carpenter from Tendring where he lived in lodgings, and he fell in love with the daughter of his landlady. The girl, Charlotte Emms, actually lived for most of the time in Shepherd's Bush as she was a cook in London and earned £28 per year – a quite reasonable wage for such a situation at the time.

The couple became engaged, but then the engagement was suddenly broken off by Hunt. The Emms family brought the case to the High Court in London, where it was found that the couple had been legally engaged. Then it was transferred to the Court of Elegit at Chelmsford for an assessment of damages. There it was revealed that the marriage had been called off due to the opposition of Hunt's parents; his mother was not happy because Charlotte Emms was marked by smallpox, a disease about which a lot of people still held unsound ideas at the time.

One witness felt that it was entirely the mother's fault: 'I don't think his mother will let him marry anybody. It seems to be the mother who has frightened him,' the witness said. Miss Emms was awarded £25 damages.

Bigamy was also quite common, though this actually counted as a criminal offence whereas 'Breach of Promise' was a civil one. There were two types of bigamist – one who simply got married again with the sure knowledge that the previous partner was still alive, and one who got married after being separated for years and with the assumption that the other partner had died.

William Hampking was typical of the second type, for he had not heard of his previous wife for 4 years when he remarried in 1861. Nonetheless he was punished with 6 weeks hard labour. In 1862 a singularly unlikely case arose in Brentwood. Mrs Wilson of Brentwood was tried at Bow Street for bigamy. She had first married Captain Le Hunte Wilson, and then married the unlikely-named Jonathan Gotobed at Brentwood Catholic Chapel. It was rumoured that Gotobed was also already married to a woman in America! Unfortunately Essex sources do not record what the verdict was.

Punishment for bigamy could be severe. In 1899 a 60 year old Colchester man was given 4 years in prison for bigamy. This compares to a case in Clacton in 1890, when shoemaker William Baldry illegally married his aunt; he was given only six weeks in prison.

Comparatively rare were civil actions brought for seduction. In March 1851 a brewer from Ware, Hertfordshire, brought an action against Isaac Rist for seducing his daughter Ruth. Rist was a grocer's assistant, and by March 1851 had moved to Maldon leaving Ruth with a child. As a respectable tradesman, the brewer would have been hoping to secure an advantageous marriage for his daughter, but her pregnancy would have ruined all chance of this. Rist had been paying three shillings a week towards the upkeep of the child, but this was not enough to satisfy the brewer Page. Courtroom dialogue was reported in detail, the local press having a field day with the descriptions of the relationship:

> 'The woman admitted that there had been no promise of marriage and that the intimacy had been going on for two years before she found herself pregnant.'

Damages were awarded against Rist of £50.

Elopement cases also tended to attract popular interest. For much of the Victorian period all the property held by a married couple was deemed to belong to the husband, so whenever a woman ran off, her paramour was liable to be charged with theft. This happened in the Canvey Island elopement case, where Walter Walford was accused of stealing four beds, twelve chairs, five tables, three clothes boxes, one chest of drawers, one clock and sundry household goods from William Pickmore on 26th September 1881. The charge hid the fact that Walford had run off with Mrs Pickmore, clearing the house of everything they possibly could!

The Pickmores had been married for 25 years – each was aged about 50. Walford was their lodger and, as tended to happen when extra men were available, Mrs Pickmore became 'too familiar' with Walford. Her husband noticed that their relationship was becoming rather tender for a landlady/lodger relationship, and a number of marital rows resulted from his attempts to correct his errant wife. In August 1881, Pickmore went away to work on the harvest, not returning home until 30th September.

Whilst Pickmore had been off cutting the corn, his wife and Walford had been making hay while the sun shone. Pickmore returned to find that 'every vestige' of furniture and clothing had been removed from his home. It didn't take much imagination for him to work out what had happened, and he soon found out that

Walford and his wife had loaded a railway truck at Benfleet station a few days earlier. The Police were called in, and the eloping couple traced to Mitcham in Surrey, where they were discovered to be living as man and wife with the contents of Pickmore's home.

Walford was brought back to Essex and tried for theft. During the trial the judge had to censure the officer guarding Walford for not controlling him properly. Walford's defence tried to argue that Pickmore was the guilty party, claiming that it was he who had left his wife. This nonsense was quite rightly ignored, and Walford was given six months in prison. When the sentence was declared, Mrs Pickmore, 'a woman apparently 50 years of age, rushed up to the prisoner, threw her arms around his neck, and kissed him.' This scene caused the judge even further annoyance!

Another case that nearly ended with the men involved being sent to prison was the 1886 Colchester elopement case. This involved two young women, Florence Nightingale Mills, who was 19, and a Miss Church. The two young women formed a relationship with two soldiers of the Essex Regiment band, and 'kept company' as the Victorian phrase went. One day Mr Mills, father of Florence, returned home to find his house locked – which was unusual. When he succeeded in forcing entry he found the place in chaos; £9 and some valuables were missing.

Mr Mills' first thought was that the house had been burgled, but then he was struck by the absence of his daughter and her clothes. The landlady of the 'Beehive' had seen Florence and some young men go to Hythe station in a cab, so the chase commenced. One of the soldiers, Frederick Stanley, was caught at the station in possession of some of the stolen property, but the other three escaped.

Stanley was found to have several envelopes containing pieces of wedding cake in his pockets. The luggage was also found at the station, and one of the ladies' packages contained an 'Ever Young Bridal Bouquet Bloom'. Shortly afterwards the other soldier, Frank Holland, was caught, but the two girls got away.

The two soldiers could have been tried for theft but Mr Mills decided to drop the charges against them as he felt the two girls were equally to blame.

Once people were married, things did not always go well. Some men simply abandoned their families, which was a criminal offence in itself – not because the law cared for the distraught family, but because they would become a burden on the local Poor

Law rates! Assault or attempted murder was common between husband and wife, or vice versa, especially as there was no prospect of divorce for the poor.

Emma Hume of Tollesbury was only 24, but she was married to a man who was quite old. Why she had married him in the first place is not recorded, but she soon attempted to end the marriage with a dose of poison. Her husband developed a 'very sickly appearance' on account of the pills of 'sugar of lead' which she had been giving him on the excuse that they would cure his liver complaint. She was transported for life in 1847.

Another romance with the lodger ended in court in January 1882. William Marvin was the lodger of James Cole of Langham for much of 1881, but Cole eventually threw him out as Marvin was getting far too friendly with Mrs Cole. Early in December Mrs Cole left her husband, doubtless to visit Marvin who had moved to Colchester, but returned again a fortnight later.

One Saturday night a few days later, Cole went out into his yard and was surprised to see Marvin looking in through his window. There was a scuffle in the yard and the husband was knocked to the ground. The frustrated lover started to go, but then turned round and hit out at the husband again, this time using his own fabrication of a 'life preserver'. The *Essex Standard* reported that this was 'apparently a very curiously made and murderous weapon'. Marvin's one was a piece of twisted wire, about a foot long, which was rather elastic and loaded at one end with a heavy knob of lead. The knob of lead came into contact with the husband's head on two occasions, as a result of which the violent Romeo ended up receiving nine months hard labour. His defence, that he had returned to collect 10s 10d that was owed to him was rejected.

Jealousy played a part in many a marital row. At Colchester Artillery Barracks in 1886 it nearly led to the death of a wife. John Price was known as a steady sort of fellow and a teetotaller, but he overheard a conversation between his wife and his sister which led him to believe that his wife was being unfaithful. He gave vent to his feelings in a verbal assault on the two women, but they attacked him. The women tried to push him into a bedroom, but Price picked up a carving knife and stabbed his wife twice. She was taken to hospital but was not considered to be in any great danger. Local sympathy was for Price: 'He is said to have led an unhappy life with his wife, who it is alleged had greatly neglected her home and her children.'

2. Indecent Behaviour

Though the Victorian press loved to report a murder in the most gruesome detail, it was rather more circumspect where 'indecency' was involved. Cases were usually referred to in the barest detail, such as the three Dunmow men who were each fined five shillings in 1862 for 'molesting' a 13 year old girl. Henry Rice was charged with committing an 'indecent act' upon a 15 year old in 1882, whilst 4 years later Richard Thake was given 3 months hard labour for 'assault' upon a Thaxted girl. The same year John Brand of Epping was given 8 months hard labour for criminal assault on a 13 year old. Very occasionally homosexuals were also brought to court, their crime usually being referred to as 'an unnatural offence'. Another offence was 'committing an unnatural act with an animal'; several cases of this were brought during Victorian times, but there were few convictions – presumably because the second party to the act was unable to give evidence.

The Age of Consent laws were involved in a number of indecency cases, though under the Criminal Law Amendment Acts intercourse by an adult with a young girl was considered a criminal assault. Until 1875 the age of consent was only 12, and then it was raised – after much debate – to 13. Ten years later it was raised to the present level. The laws were as necessary then as they are now – in fact they were probably more necessary in Victorian times when 'white slavery' was a real problem. Totally typical of these cases was that of John Izzard, aged 60, who was charged at the Summer Assizes of 1870 with criminally assaulting a girl under 12 (then the minimum age). He committed the act at Harlow. The punishment was 15 months hard labour. At the same Assize, two 15 year old farm boys from Clavering (again!) were given 12 and 15 months hard labour respectively for attempted rape.

The seduction of young women and the pressing of them into prostitution became a concern of the more philanthropic members of the Victorian middle classes, and some of them formed societies to fight the moral battle. The National Society for the Prevention of Cruelty to Children was involved in a number of cases around Britain later in the century, but one case that involved Essex was prosecuted by the Society for the Suppression of Vice in 1872. The case was tried at Ilford and involved Catherine Pusey, a girl from Silvertown. John Ross was accused of abducting her without her parents' consent, the girl being under 16. Joseph Stephens, a local gatekeeper had become aware of the girl's potential and he arranged a meeting between her and John Ross. Stephens was undoubtedly paid for this service. Ross was clearly a man practised in the art of seducing younger women, for his treatment of Pusey is typical of the 'modus operandi' of young rakes of the day. He took her to North Woolwich gardens, then very fashionable, then took her into London by first class train. They spent an evening at the music hall then shared a bed at a coffee house. The next day the girl returned home, but didn't tell her mother the full story until Ross failed to turn up for their next meeting, by which time she feared pregnancy. Ross defended himself by saying the girl claimed to be 17. His punishment was not recorded.

Sometimes the law as it stood appeared unfair to Victorian juries, who would hesitate to convict a man of criminal assault or abducting a girl if they thought that the girl had encouraged him in his actions. This was the situation when George Richardson, a young Bocking matmaker, was charged in 1892 with abducting 15 year old Florence Mott. The two young lovers had disappeared off to Colchester together, where they had asked for 'a bed for two' at the *Bee Hive Inn*. Florence's mother had to go and fetch her from Colchester, something she wasn't unfamiliar with as she had previously had to collect her daughter from Colchester Police Station. When Richardson was brought to trial, the *Essex Standard* reported that '. . . the girl looks several years older than she actually is. She is said to be advanced in pregnancy.' Richardson was then remanded, and the Assize deferred judgement in his case.

The whole area of immorality and indecency was, of course, the field of the blackmailer. Blackmail cases rarely got into the papers unless a victim had the courage to take on the troublemakers. One man who was not prepared to be blackmailed was Joseph Robson, a partner in a large Saffron Walden retail business. Robson was a happily married man and a Quaker as well, but two women decided to try and extort money from him by alleging that the three of them had committed immoral acts together. A number of threatening letters were sent by the women, Anne Hurry and Jane Bradford, but Robson resisted. He fought and won a slander case

A convicted criminal serving a term of hard labour.

to clear his name, then received a letter asking him to meet his blackmailers on the common at 9pm. He did just that – but ensured that the Superintendent of Police was watching. The two women were arrested and given 9 months hard labour each.

Rape was regarded as a most serious offence, but still tended to be punished with less severe sentences than crimes against property. Colchester rapist William Douglas received only 2 years hard labour in 1848 for a most brutal and callous attack on a young woman; this compares to a sentence at about the same time of seven years transportation for burglary. The event occurred when Agnes Lewin, a servant, arrived at Colchester railway station one evening but couldn't find a cab to take her home. Douglas, a railway porter, offered to help her get a cab and escorted Miss Lewin to the *Waggon & Horses* pub. There they got the cab driven by James Keys, into which Lewin clambered – to be followed, much to her surprise, by Douglas. 'She called out and resisted to the utmost of her powers; but afterwards became insensible.' This crime was treated as less serious than a minor theft.

Rape cases were notoriously difficult to prove, a situation which has continued to this day. In Victorian times the victim of rape was treated to very little privacy, and injured women were likely to have their personal details discussed in the court-room. One woman who had this experience was Ann Eades of Bocking, who brought an action for rape against George Metson in 1852. She was described as 'a good-looking woman, 18 years of age'. Both parties in the case lived in Bocking Church Street and vaguely knew each other before the day of the incident. On that day they got into conversation, and went to the *Oak* public house to drink gin. They started walking home together, but called in at the *Black Boy* on the way; Ann Eades alleged later that Metson forced her to visit this pub against her will.

From the *Black Boy* they continued walking home, but when they got to Metson's house the girl claimed that she was dragged inside and raped in a back room. She did not tell her father about the attack until the next day.

When the jury recorded a verdict of 'Not Guilty' for Metson, there was considerable surprise. They argued, though, that drink had played a part in the events. That, under the influence of alcohol, the girl had consented to intercourse, but when she had sobered up regretted what had happened. As in many rape case verdicts, opinion was divided as to whether the jury had made the right decision.

The fairly light punishment of 9 months hard labour was given to Robert Falkard, a Colchester publican, in 1862. Falkard was the owner of the *Flying Fox* public house, who drank too much himself; on one occasion he got into a drunken fury and threw his wife out, then turned his attention to Eliza Cook the servant girl, aged 13. The girl fled upstairs to her room and tied the door shut with string, but Falkard forced his way in and raped her twice. Eventually the girl escaped to the house of a nearby policeman and the publican was arrested.

The degree of punishment awarded seems to have been very arbitrary, often seeming to depend on the impression given as to the resistance of the victim. Where small children were involved the punishments were likely to be more severe.

William Harborn, aged 56, had to seek the protection of the Police after raping a three year old child at Chelmsford in 1863. Harborn was a weaver, and came across the child playing in the street; he led her into a field where the offence was committed, the child being found later in Moulsham. A mob discovered the identity of the rapist before the Police, and Harborn was forced to give himself up to the Police before the mob got hold of him.

A particularly heinous assault on a small girl was committed by Charles Minter in Colchester in the same year. Minter ran a baker's shop and one of his customers was an 11 year old girl. Minter took the girl upstairs, where the attack took place, but threatened her with violence so strongly that the girl told no one for months. It was only when the girl was found to be suffering from 'a loathsome disease' that the parents discovered the truth. They immediately went to see Minter, who offered to come to an 'arrangement' with them. Colchester was shocked by the case, though the local press drew a veil over the court proceedings: 'The evidence, which was of a most disgusting nature, occupied the Court for some time . . .' Minter was punished with 10 years in prison. It was a sad fact that many Victorians believed that some forms of venereal disease could be cured by intercourse with a young girl, and this appears to have been the motive for Minter's assault.

3. The Treatment of Children

In an age when contraception was not generally available, unwanted pregnancies were a common occurrence. These could afflict unmarried girls and also married couples, for children were expensive to feed.

The murder of children was thus quite commonplace. It must also be assumed that a fair number of child or baby murders never reached the courts as they were not detected in an age of erratic medical treatment. The usual sort of situation was that of Elizabeth Biss of Harlow, who killed her baby with a blow to the head and left its body at Harlow Pond in 1838. Mrs Biss had a bad reputation in the district, as she was living apart from her husband and 'keeping a house of not very reputable connexions on the London Road.'

Earl's Colne was rocked by rumours of child murder in April 1847, but the Coroner eventually concluded that the child had died from inflammation of the stomach. The Coroner also observed, however, that the child had been disgracefully neglected, and the circumstances of its brief life reveal a little about the conditions of life in a poor family. The father of the child was a man named Banyard, a blacksmith, who shared a bed with Miss

Porter, the child's mother, and Mrs Porter, the grandmother. Under these appalling conditions, Miss Porter seems to have made no effort to care for the child at all, not possessing a single article of clothing for the child. After it was born in March 1847 it was put to sleep on a pile of old clothes laid across two chairs. Several days later it was observed to be yellow and bruised, dying within a month of its birth. The child murder rumour came about because it was alleged that the grandmother had been seen buying 'sugar of lead' from a local shop, but the Coroner ruled out poisoning.

A sad case of child murder occurred at Romford in 1851. The whole incident was observed by a ten year old boy, who happened to be looking in the window when it happened. He saw Esther Playle, mother of the child, sitting on a sofa and appearing to play with the child. She called it over to her, took it onto her lap and, to the boy's astonishment, cut its throat with a razor. She then threw it up to the ceiling, the small child crying 'Oh mother'. Mrs Playle's last words to her dying child were, 'Open the door and let the stink out.' She was found to be insane.

Concealing a birth was an offence closely related to child murder, since many mothers kept their pregnancy secret in the hope of disposing of a child when it was born. The law against 'concealment' applied equally to fully developed pregnancies and to miscarriages. Ann Mead of Navestock was given one month hard labour for concealing a birth in 1851 even though she had only been three months pregnant. She was a servant girl, a class who had more to lose through illegitimate pregnancy than most others since it invariably led to loss of employment. Mead gave birth after only three months, the child being stillborn. Instead of sending for the doctor she cut the child up into several pieces with the dinner knives. Part of the child was put down the privy in the garden, and the remainder down the water closet in the house. Mead came close to being tried for child murder as it was alleged that the child had been born alive, but there was no evidence apart from her own word on this point.

Another servant girl to be prosecuted for concealing a birth was Ellen Venus of Great Clacton, whose surname was the opportunity for local reporters to make puns about the 'goddess of love'. She was an unmarried woman who had previously worked for Reverend Bishops. The child seems to have been stillborn, and then disposed of in typical fashion by being put down the privy. She was given 12 months hard labour.

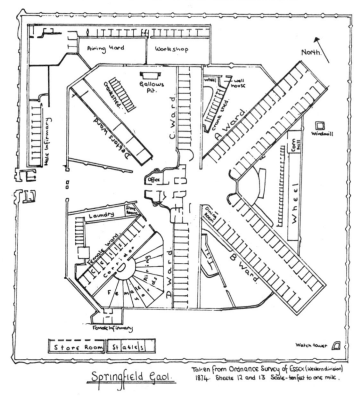

A plan of Springfield gaol. It contains several features characteristic of the period, including the cranksheds where convicts would be set to grinding and hopeless work.

Esther Bishop, tried for child murder in Colchester in 1882, was also a servant. She was a widow and earned her keep through being in service to Colonel Black of the South Wales Borderers. She became pregnant and gave birth without telling anyone; shortly after this she placed the baby in a copper containing five inches of water, as a result of which it drowned. A verdict of 'Not Guilty' on the charge of child murder was recorded, but she was given fifteen months hard labour for concealment of birth.

Civil actions for an 'order of affiliation' were often brought against various young men who had got girls into trouble and then attempted to ditch them. In 1851 Mary Ann Kent of Wivenhoe brought such an action against William Howling, described as a mariner. Kent was 'a young woman of defective understanding'. Howling was ordered to pay two shillings a week to maintain the child.

4. Prostitution

The biggest issue over prostitution in Victorian Essex was the political debate concerning the Contagious Diseases Acts of 1864, 1866 and 1869. These Acts were a response to the belief that venereal diseases were rife in the armed forces and allowed the Police in certain garrison towns like Colchester to inspect women suspected of being prostitutes and to detain them in hospital if they were diseased. The Acts infuriated the champions of women's rights, and in 1869 a campaign was started by Mrs Josephine Butler to have them repealed. She visited Colchester during the 1870 election to campaign on the issue, and ran into quite a lot of opposition.

Prostitution was certainly, therefore, an issue in Victorian society but very little was known about it. Most towns in Victorian Essex would have had a few prostitutes, like the Harlow child murderer mentioned above, but more common were the girls in poorly paid jobs who were prepared to earn a little extra through occasional prostitution.

Some of the habitual prostitutes ended up in court regularly, often charged with offences such as being drunk or using profane language in the street. Ellen Prentice was one such Colchester woman. She appeared before the Magistrates in 1874 for being 'riotous' in Head Street, and was described as 'a young woman of loose character'. She was given 14 days hard labour. This sort of case occurred frequently.

As has been mentioned above, the Criminal Law Amendment Acts were used to raise the 'age of consent' in order to deter child prostitution. The raising of this age was due to a combined effort by Josephine Butler, the Salvation Army, and W.T. Stead, the editor of the *Pall Mall Gazette*. Stead wrote a series of articles to expose the white slave trade, which he called 'The Maiden Tribute of Modern Babylon'. The articles landed him in gaol but the age of consent was raised to 16 a month later.

One of the first cases in the country to be brought under the new legislation involved a part of Essex that is now considered to be in London. William Carr, aged 25, was charged with attempting felonious assault upon Matilda French, aged 15, at Plaistow in 1886. Matilda French came from Tiptree. Also in court was Matilda's sister Martha, charged with keeping a girl for unlawful purposes contrary to the Criminal Law Amendment Act of 1885, section six. Martha French's mother believed that her older daughter was married to Carr, and had allowed Matilda to go to London to stay with them whilst seeking employment. Instead, Martha French and Carr had virtually imprisoned the girl and forced her to work as a prostitute. In addition, all three shared the same bed and Carr had frequently assaulted Matilda, who was under the legal age of 16.

Martha French was acquitted, but Carr received 20 months hard labour. Nonetheless, this was an historic case.

Some charitable organisations attempted to protect children from vice, especially where parental neglect was concerned. In 1890 the NSPCC was active around Chelmsford and brought several cases, not all of which worked out successfully. One girl, aged 15, was taken to a Home as she was considered to be in moral danger. This Home was out of Chelmsford, but the girl had to be brought back to Chelmsford for the legal hearings. When she returned she was met by her mother and a host of other women, who 'liberated' the girl from her guardians and spirited her off into Chelmsford's slums. It was not unknown for parents to encourage their daughters to be involved in vice.

It must be said that Victorian Essex showed a curious and ambivalent attitude to moral questions. On the one hand crimes like rape were punished much more lightly than crimes against property, on the other hand much was made of the need for high moral standards. Women in particular suffered from this, and were frequently subjected to humiliation in and out of the courts. It seems also to have been the rule that a woman was invariably guilty until proved innocent, even if she was the victim rather than the criminal.

As a final example of this double-faced Victorianism, we may take the extraordinary trial of Stephen Rudland in 1865. Rudland was a young man who was charged with burglary and rape against Jane Marriott at Great Chesterford. The two lived quite near each other and had been acquainted for nine years, stretching back into Rudland's childhood. Marriott was quite a few years older than him, and at the time of the incident was a widow with five children. She had once given Rudland supper at her house, and the young man seems to have become obsessed with her. On the night of the incident, Rudland's passion was such that he broke into Marriott's house through the bakehouse window and she awoke to hear footsteps ascending the stairs. She shouted out at the intruder, but Rudland said, 'It's only me', and she recognised his voice. She objected to his being there quite forcefully; this was the second time he'd broken in as the previous week she had found him asleep downstairs.

Rudland refused to leave however, and instead took off his trousers and got into bed. She promptly got out the other side. Rudland made a grab for the woman, forced her back onto the bed, and raped her.

When the offence came to court a determined effort was made to slur Jane Marriott's character. The defence alleged that an 'improper intimacy' existed between the two and that she had invited him into her bedroom. This, the prosecution argued, was ridiculous. Marriott had merely shown kindness to Rudland in the past and, if she invited him in, why had he broken the bakehouse window in order to force entry?

In his summing up the judge showed considerable favour towards the prisoner, and to his obvious disgust the jury recorded a verdict of Guilty. They recommended mercy to the judge, who reacted sarcastically. 'If you have found him guilty of a charge like this, why do you recommend mercy?' The Foreman of the Jury replied that, 'The Jury think the prosecutrix might have used more resistance.' Rudland was given 5 years penal servitude, but it was a curious philosophy that dictated that the punishment of a rapist should depend on how much resistance the female victim was prepared to risk making, especially when she had small children in the house.

INCENDIARISM

~~~◇~~~

INCENDIARISM was the Victorian word for arson. In a county where much of the wealth derived from the land, and all the power was wielded by the great landowners, incendiarism was regarded as a horrifying crime because it struck against a farmer and his property. It was a notoriously difficult crime to prevent as well; a farmer, deep in the countryside and with many unguarded barns and haystacks, was always going to be prone to the attacks of the arsonist. Once a fire had been started, help would take a long time to arrive, by which time severe destruction might have been caused. The judges of Victorian Essex therefore felt it necessary to have deterrent punishments for incendiarists, and as late as 1829 a boy was executed for the crime.

When William May was tried for arson in March 1840 the judge told the Court at the start of the trial that it was a very severe offence that, until recently, had been punishable with death. On 12th October 1839 an oats stack was set on fire at Lubbards Lodge Farm near Rayleigh, which belonged to Daniel Brown. The fire started at about 9pm and rapidly spread to engulf four other stacks and some buildings. The damage was severe, the destruction amounting to £500 worth of corn, £500 of buildings and £150 of farm implements.

William May had worked for Brown for 20 years, since he was 13. He lived about 1½ miles away from the farm, and on the night in question had gone out to the chemist's shop to buy some matches. He had returned to his lodgings at midnight, when the landlord had told him that there was a fire at Brown's; May refused to go with the landlord to see it. May was arrested and found guilty of arson; he had also been convicted for stealing rabbits. He was transported for life.

There were two main reasons for incendiarist attacks. One was that it was a frequent method of repaying a grudge – either by a discontented worker or by a tramp who had been rudely turned away; the other reason was that in an age when farmworkers had little political muscle it was one way of compensating for the failure of early trade unions.

The more 'political' causes of incendiarism have been written about by Malcolm Baker in an excellent little pamphlet called *The Revolt of the Field*. Mr Baker felt that incendiarism was most prevalent in northern Essex from 1830 up to the later 1850s, with particular outbreaks in 1843–4 and 1848–9.

The first severe outbreak was at West Bergholt in 1842–4, with over a dozen fires being started. These mostly occurred between the harvest and the following spring, when the farmer would have most to lose. Five different farmers were attacked, thus emphasising that a personal grudge was not the cause of this outbreak. Robert Woodward, an unemployed labourer, was eventually arrested for the crimes and transported for life.

There were a few incidents around the county in late 1843, but there was then a major outbreak of incendiarism at Ardleigh on the night of 29th January 1844. £1,300 damage was caused by four separate fires, which were clearly part of an organised attack. According to the *Ipswich Journal*, many labourers were 'openly exalting in the progress of the fires' and so local landowners combined to offer rewards. A few months later there was a similar outbreak in the Tendring district. By Spring 1844 fires were breaking out around Braintree and Halstead. Very few criminals were caught during this spate of incendiarism, the only major punishments being the transporting for life of two Ardleigh men in March 1845.

After this incendiarism became less common. It perhaps ceased to be an 'epidemic' and returned to its normal state of being 'endemic'. Incidents became more isolated, such as the February 1847 attack on Naylinghurst Farm near Braintree, where a £300 stack of wheat was destroyed.

There was a major fire at Hall Farm, Wickham Bishops, on the night of 2nd April 1851. Three sheds, two barns, a granary and an ox-house were destroyed; a number of animals died too, including 17 bullocks and some sheep. All the property belonged to Thomas Smith. Suspicion immediately centred on Benjamin Wager, but he

Essex Stocks, kept as a warning to troublemakers.

disappeared and was not caught until October 1852. Wager had been a casual labourer on Smith's farm but had been refused regular work, so held a grudge against the farmer. He had wanted to lodge at the 'Ragged House', the farm and barn complex that was destroyed in the fire, but Smith had refused this too. About 6 weeks before the fire, Wager had told another labourer that, 'If Mr Smith would not let him lodge at the Ragged House he would do the old b—— a turn.' Wager said that he would attack Smith at night, but in the event he confined his assault to Smith's property.

When he was eventually arrested, Wager accused another labourer, Jim Ewers, of being the incendiarist. Ewers' mother was able to state that he had returned home at 10.50pm on the night of the fire and had been in a sober condition, whilst the fire was known to have been started at some time after 11pm. Moreover Wager, who was arrested in Hatfield, had been seen hanging around the Ragged Barn on the night of the fire. He was given 14 years transportation.

A more unusual type of arson occurred in 1852, or so the Sun Fire Office alleged. They claimed that farmer John Nodes of Bardfield set fire to his own barn and cow-house in order to defraud them of the insurance money. Nodes had originally insured the buildings for £15 and £100 respectively, but a few days before the fire renewed his insurance at £100 and £200 for each building. This seemed very suspicious to the insurance company, but the jury were not convinced and Nodes were found not guilty.

The early 1860s seem to have been a bad time for incendiarism. John Savill set fire to a stack at Ivy Farm, Little Dunmow, in 1862 in a desperate attempt to draw attention to his own plight. Having started the fire with a lucifer match, he made no attempt to escape and simply stood there watching the blaze. When questioned, he admitted being the arsonist and said he had done it because he wanted to be sent out of the country; 'I had better be transported then be in the Union all my life.' By 'the Union' he meant the workhouse, so he clearly committed the crime when depressed about being continually unemployed — lack of work was a problem in the agricultural districts at the time. Savill did not get his wish though, for he was sentenced to 6 years penal servitude so that he wasn't transported.

There were several cases of arson at the Lent Assizes of March 1862. One involved an 11 year old boy, James Digby, who was accused of setting fire to three haystacks at Great Leighs. The boy said that he had been hunting for rabbits and had gone amongst the haystacks; there he had struck a match against his trousers and caused the fire by accident. He was acquitted. Not so lucky was Arthur Templeton, who pleaded guilty to setting fire to a haystack at Chelmsford; he was given 15 years penal servitude.

The spate of incendiarism continued into 1863, and the Winter Assizes that year again included several cases. John McCube, a watch spring maker, was already known to have started a fire at Rochford when he set light to a stack of corn worth £79 at South Weald. He was arrested almost immediately and found to be carrying matches. Sentence was 3 years penal servitude, interestingly much less than Templeton had received! Also tried was William Griggs for a fire at Stansted Mountfichet in December 1863. Griggs had bought some lucifer matches at the *Kings Arms* that evening, and was present at the fire. Whilst watching the blaze he observed to another man that 'Whoever did it ought to be chucked into it'. He was found not guilty through lack of evidence.

The Lent Assizes of 1866 also featured a couple of cases. One of these was a 'timid-looking child', who was in fact John Everett, aged 8. He had set fire to a stack at Rainham, but the court gave him over to his father to deal with. More serious was the case of William Taylor, who was found guilty of arson at Radwinter and given 10 years penal servitude. Taylor had arrived at Isaac Saward's farm in early February, saying that he was destitute, and had been given work and allowed to sleep in the stable. On the day of the fire Taylor bought a box of 'Vesuvian' matches, and that evening the stable was discovered to be in flames. The fire spread from there to engulf two barns, a cart lodge, and a cottage. Some barley and wheat were destroyed, with total damages amounting to over £400. Taylor had previously been in gaol for stealing a watch, and appears to have started the fire because he had formed a grudge against Saward. It was for just this sort of reason that farmers were afraid of wandering labourers, though if you turned one away without work they were also likely to return to start a fire.

Some arsonists were undoubtedly insane. One such was George Clark, a middle-aged baker, who was arrested for a fire at Moreton in 1870. In the dock he behaved very strangely indeed, and so was acquitted on grounds of insanity.

In the early 1870s there was a strong movement towards the formation of trade unions for agricultural workers in Essex. Not surprisingly, some of the farmers were quick to blame any fires on union activity. Thus in 1874 the Kelvedon branch of the labourers' union sent out a circular denouncing arson as a weapon in their struggle; working class protest had moved into a new phase, but feelings still ran high.

Incendiarism as a means of hitting back at a farmer died out towards the end of the century. It became more commonly known as 'arson' and tended after that time to be the preserve of the deranged or the lunatic; 'grudge' fires became quite rare.

RIOT!

❧ ◇ ❧

THE British like to think themselves as a quiet, well-behaved race, which is why they react with such horror to scenes of riot on their streets. The truth, though, is rather different. For centuries riot has been a frequent occurrence in our towns and cities. In fact there were times in the past when it was possible to predict when riots would occur with considerable ease. This chapter looks at a few types of riot that were a problem in Victorian Essex.

1. Election Riots

Violence at an election has almost disappeared from the British political way of life in the 1980s, but in Victorian Essex there were riots at most elections. Usually these involved a few skirmishes between supporters of the contending parties, but occasionally things got worse; in Britain as a whole it was not uncommon for people to be killed during elections. Strangely the degree of violence involved was in inverse proportion to the number of people who could vote, and as the various Reform Acts extended the electorate so the amount of violence at elections declined.

Riots did not only occur at the major towns of the County. The election of 4th December 1885 produced a number of incidents in Castle Hedingham where fierce political loyalties and strong drink combined to cause a rough night for the local Police. Most of the trouble occurred at the village's hostelries, like the *Wheat Sheaf* where a bar-room fight broke out. The Police arrived and succeeded in ejecting one of the troublemakers, but John Smith proved more of a problem. He smashed some gas-light fittings in his fury before the Police triumphed. Arthur Pannel got annoyed with beer-house keeper Thomas Radley, with politics being the issue, and broke his windows. He was fined £1.

These incidents were minor, but the history of Colchester is dotted with more serious electoral disturbances. 1852 saw an electoral contest between W. Hawkins, Hardcastle, Lord John Manners and Prinsep, that ended with considerable chaos in the town's High Street. When the dust had settled, the local press put the blame on the Essex Police, a detachment of whom had been brought into Colchester for the occasion under the command of Captain MacHardy who had been appointed the first Chief Constable of Essex in 1840. Colchester had its own Police, and there was considerable local feeling in the town against MacHardy's intruders.

MacHardy's Police arrived in Colchester to help supervise the declaration of the result. This was always a troublesome occasion as thousands of rival supporters gathered in the High Street to hear the result and boo their enemies. There was no secret ballot in those days, so the crowd would know in advance which party a particular dignitary supported and would voice their feelings in accordance. These events had traditionally involved some individual fighting in the crowd, and occasionally missiles were thrown, but it was expected that the Borough's Police would be able to control these routine problems. The presence of MacHardy's officers, though, was seen by many as a provocative gesture. At the time members of the 'Establishment' were just as likely to be anti-Police as the lower classes.

As the time for the declaration of the result drew near, there were about 6,000 people gathered in the High Street. As normal, 'a number of pugilistic encounters took place', but the scores of Borough and County Police did nothing to intervene or stop the fights. 'Scores of rural and borough constables were held in a compact body under the hustings', it was reported. When a priest asked a superintendent why nothing was done to put a stop to the fighting, he was told to mind his own business.

Then the game of baiting the opposition began in the crowd. Two election banners belonging to partisan local magistrates were paraded down the High Street; these were attacked and torn up by the angry opponents. Amidst an atmosphere of heavy drinking, a fierce assault was made by the crowd on the blue banners of the Tory Party. The result was declared, announcing that Hawkins and Manners were elected, but not Hardcastle and Prinsep.

The crude wooden hustings erected in Colchester for a by-election. It is easy to imagine how it could be torn down when a crowd got out of control on these occasions.

At this point MacHardy's Police assaulted the crowd; 120 officers waded into the throng, laying about them blindly with heavy wooden staves. The assault seemed to have no particular purpose as a mere three or four persons were arrested, but a number received injuries. Reaction of the strongly-Tory *Essex Standard* revealed the feelings of many of those present:

> 'We have never before witnessed in this town a combined and undistinguishing onslaught of Police on the assembled electors.'

The Police, the newspaper stated, had simply attacked the crowd as a whole,

> '. . . dealing their merciless blows in every direction, inflicting wounds alike on the obstreperous and the peaceable.'

The 1870 Colchester election also saw scenes of lamentable behaviour. Following the death in October 1870 of sitting MP Gordon Rebow, Sir Henry Storks attempted to win the seat for the Liberals who were then in Government. The seat was eventually won by a Tory, Colonel Learmouth, by a margin of 400 votes. A key issue in the battle was Government legislation that allowed women suspected of being prostitutes to be inspected for venereal diseases. This was considered to be a severe infringement of women's legal rights, and a Doctor Baxter Langley stood against Storks on a platform of getting the legislation repealed. Langley was helped in his campaigning by the redoubtable Josephine Butler, who was followed everywhere by a gang of toughs so that on one occasion she had to be smuggled out of a hotel when the toughs lay in wait for her.

The candidates each took up residence at a particular hotel which then served as a base for their supporters. Colonel Learmouth stayed at the *Cups* and Storks at the *Red Lion*; the latter was troubled by rival supporters who would gather outside his hotel, booing loudly. Another candidate, Sangster, stood for the 'Association for Revivers of British Industry'.

The various meetings held during the 1870 campaign were characterised by rowdy behaviour. The Working Men's Liberal Association organised a meeting in Magdalen Street, to which a large 'rough element' turned out. When various people clambered on to a waggon to speak they were deluged with rotten apples thrown by ill-mannered Conservatives. Another working-class meeting in the Public Hall, organised by Sangster's supporters, degenerated into a free fight as the other parties' supporters took over the platform.

In June 1886 there were similar chaotic scenes in Colchester. Radicals attacked the Tory Club and smashed its windows and 'blue waggons' were pelted with eggs and coloured powders. This appears to have been a rare instance of the Tories doing badly out of the election fights. There were a number of drunken brawls, especially involving one at the 'Woolpack' in Saint Botolph's Street where one Police Constable found himself having to deal with a violent crowd of over two hundred excited campaigners.

2. Salvation Army Riots

Of course the Salvation Army itself never went on a riot, but its appearance on the streets of Essex in the latter part of the 19th Century provoked strong feelings on the part of some of the population. A number of persons tried to put paid to the Salvation Army by a campaign of riotous behaviour. The problem got so bad that in 1885–6 Colchester Corporation tried to introduce byelaws to stop the Salvation Army parading on Saturdays and

Sundays, but these bye-laws were rejected by the Home Secretary. A number of Councils, though, did pursue legal measures against the Salvationists and in one South Coast resort an entire Band was locked up in the Police cells to stop them parading.

Harwich was one of the first towns in Essex where trouble broke out. During the early part of 1882 the Salvationists took to parading the streets there, and trouble resulted. In April a local reporter was able to write that there had been 'several collisions between the members of the Salvation Army parading the streets and a number of roughs, and some disgraceful scenes have occurred'. The Harwich Watch Committee decided to stop people from congregating in the streets, but this measure was of doubtful legality and provided no solution.

Within a few days the trouble was brought to court when Robert Felgate was charged with an assault on Corporal Joseph Lines of the Salvation Army. On 16th April 1882 the Army had been intercepted in Church Street by the roughs, one of whom had struck Lines on the head with a stick and knocked him out. Defence counsel tried to pin the blame on the Army, saying that their 'tactics' drew a crowd together and encouraged riot. He even alleged that the Salvationist Captain had been the first to strike a blow: the Captain, Thomas Gibson, was also charged with assault but the case was later dropped.

In their defence the Salvationists were able to show that they had stopped using a drum on their parades as it was considered provocative, and now only sang. It was proved that the trouble had started when a young man rode a horse into their ranks quite deliberately. The Army won, and Felgate was given one month's hard labour.

By 1886 the Salvation Army had spread out over most of the county. In January that year there was trouble at Brightlingsea where a 'sea lad', Alfred Morris, received a 15 shilling fine for his behaviour. He had gone along to a service but had made a lot of noise, been abusive to the Captain, had struck matches during the service, and refused to leave.

The most intense struggle seems to have been played out in Braintree. A major disturbance occurred there on 15th December 1889, when the Army were holding a service at the Public Hall in New Street. There was riotous behaviour in the street during the service, and the windows of the Public Hall were smashed by

The Braintree town lock-up in New Street, which was used to house wrong-doers in the town's more riotous past.

missiles. Ten men appeared in the dock in January 1890 as a result of this and put up a strong, but erroneous, defence. In their opinion, which they stated forcefully, it was the fault of the Police and the Salvation Army. They argued that the Police had caused the disturbance on the night in question, and that there had never been any trouble in the town until the Army had arrived. The magistrates were unimpressed by this nonsense, and fined each defendant after a sometimes rowdy trial that had lasted five hours. The ten guilty men refused to pay their fines and so were taken away to Springfield Gaol instead, treated as heroes by their friends.

By this time the enemies of the Salvation Army had taken to calling themselves the 'Skeleton Army'. They were back in action in Braintree later in January 1890, disturbing the outdoor services with loud noises and showers of rotten eggs. They were rumoured to be preparing a mass demonstration as soon as their friends were released from Springfield, and had their own 'terrible banner' to rival the Army's 'Blood and Fire' standard. It was said that the Skeletons had put a price on the capture of the Salvationists' banner.

During February 1890 there seemed a real danger of anarchy on the streets of Braintree. A morning service at the Public Hall was brought to a halt when the Skeletons staged a mass-invasion. The evening service was disrupted by a barrage of rotten apples, then the gas supply to the Hall was turned off and, under cover of darkness, the Skeletons moved in and overturned the furniture.

The following Sunday morning there was a battle in the Market Place with filthy refuse being thrown. When the service in the Public Hall started, sparrows were let loose and then pelted with catapaults. At last the authorities realised that there was a substantial threat to public order, and for the evening Police reinforcements were brought from Halstead under the command of Inspector Mann. The extra Police were able to eject the mob from the Hall, but they gathered in New Street and so the Police charged out of the Hall with batons drawn. The mob scattered.

As a result of this trouble, twelve persons appeared before the Magistrates in one sitting; they were mostly aged between 17 and 20. Significantly the case was brought by the Salvation Army itself, who alleged that those in the dock were the ringleaders of the Skeletons; the authorities appear to have been far too tolerant of the troublemakers, perhaps because they disliked the 'religious enthusiasm' of the Salvationists. Evidence as to how far the Skeletons organised their attacks was produced, and it was said that their banner carried a skull-and-crossbones motif. The twelve were given the choice of a fine or prison, and all chose prison; Alfred Hicks was given an extra one month's hard labour for assaulting a woman who was leading a service.

It must be said that the Salvation Army riots varied in extent throughout the County, and this must reflect the fact that certain local authorities chose to turn a blind eye to the activities of the troublemakers. Only when general public disorder threatened did they intervene. In Clacton, where General Booth's widow lived for a time, there was relative peace and quiet when the Army first made its appearance. It can be concluded that had the Skeletons launched their attacks on members of the established religion, they would have been dealt with much more severely.

3. Other Riots

Occasionally there were larger scale disturbances which had their origins in the sort of bad feelings that occasionally characterised village life. An example of this was the Ardleigh Riot of February 1882.

At the centre of the trouble was Samuel Everitt, the landlord of the *Lion & Lamb* public house. He was clearly more of a lion than a lamb, though, as his wife complained that he ill-treated her quite frequently. After over 8 years of marriage, she left Everitt on 13th February and sought shelter in the house of an unmarried green-grocer, Charles Gardiner, who lived nearby. After a couple of days separation, Mrs Everitt decided that her husband had probably had time to calm down and went back to the inn.

Her return was very brief though, because she fled back to Gardiner on 16th February 1882. Everitt believed that his wife's departure had nothing to do with his own bad behaviour, but quite a lot with the relationship between her and Gardiner. He convinced a large number of local people that Gardiner and Mrs Everitt were 'living as man and wife' and, together with his brothers, decided to teach Gardiner a lesson.

At about 7 o'clock on the evening of 22nd February, a crowd of about 50 people gathered in a field opposite Gardiner's cottage. The field belonged to one of Samuel Everitt's brothers, who was a farmer. A huge bonfire was lit, and the wind blew the sparks from this over Gardiner's cottage – which had a thatched roof. Then the crowd bombarded his house with missiles, breaking 72 panes of glass. Henry Everitt, the landlord's brother, set off flare rockets at the house. Finally, in time-honoured practice, effigies of Gardiner and Mrs Everitt were burnt on the bonfire.

The disturbances lasted for two hours. As the mob was departing, Samuel Everitt called out to the beleaguered Gardiner: 'Good night Charley; you may get your windows mended, and when you have done so we will come back and break them again.'

Gardiner was so scared by his experience that a Constable had to be instructed to guard his house and in March 1882 Samuel and Henry Everitt appeared in court. It was said that Mrs Everitt had decided to divorce her husband, but the defence tried to blacken her name by alleging an amorous relationship between herself and Gardiner. The latter had, in fact, been a long-time family friend. The Everitts were let off very leniently with a fine of £5 each.

In the same year there was a lot of trouble in Colchester between the Army and the Police. This was virtually a ritual sparring match, as soldiers had to be regularly disciplined for poor behaviour in Colchester and constables were often attacked –

there were several instances of this in 1865, for example. In July 1882 a crowd of between 50 and 100 soldiers got into a fight in Long Wyre Street. As usual drink and women were involved, for the Police had stepped in to arrest one Adelaide Ferguson for swearing but the soldiers had intervened to protect her. When the woman was taken off to the Police station there seemed a real danger that the soldiers would attack the station itself and liberate their female, something which did happen in other garrison towns during Victorian times.

A few days later two Privates in the 7th Hussars were charged with being drunk and disorderly in Head Street, Colchester, at 11.30pm. Two constables had attempted to arrest the soldiers, and had been assaulted. One soldier attacked a constable with his fists and a riding whip, whilst the other tore down a fence and threatened the Police with a piece of paling. One constable received a kick in the mouth, as a result of which he lost part of his tongue. When the case appeared before the Magistrates the soldiers were fined £2 each, with the Magistrates complaining bitterly that this was the maximum penalty permitted.

Another source of trouble were the navvies, who brought fear and trembling to all local residents during the building of the railways. The biggest problem with navvies was idleness – thus during the construction of the Maldon, Witham & Braintree Railway they caused problems when poor weather put a stop to work; then the navvies went into Witham, and terrorised the people of the town by wandering around drunk in large numbers.

Perhaps the worst Essex incident involving navvies was the 'Battle of Bradfield', though this was a well-organised battle involving some quite respectable people as well as the navvies themselves. It is a famous incident, and one typical of a number of 'railway battles' that took place around Victorian Britain.

The railway involved was the Mistley, Thorpe & Walton Railway which, ironically, was never completed due to lack of finance. Its aim was to give access to Walton from the Manningtree direction, in rivalry to the Tendring Hundred Railway which was then building a line from the Colchester direction. By April 1865 the relationship between the Railway Company and its contractor, Mr Munro, had deteriorated to a very low level and there was considerable bad feeling about the slow rate of progress being made.

It was decided that Munro should give up the contract for the works, and that a Mr Furness should replace him, but to allow for this a few financial arrangements had to be made. Firstly Furness objected to some of the materials that Munro was passing on to him as part of the arrangement and then a bill sent by Munro to the Railway Company caused a dispute. The bill was for £2,000, but the Railway's engineer, Cooke, considered that Munro had erred by putting one nought too many on the bill.

With his bill resulting in a shortfall of £1,800, Munro refused to give up the works so that Furness was unable to get started. Negotiations proved fruitless, so the Mistley, Thorpe & Walton Railway decided to remove Munro by force. They set 11th April as the date for the operation.

The Railway Company assembled their own army of 60 'lumpers' or longshoremen who were brought in from Harwich; they were led by Cooke, who the *Essex Standard* referred to as 'Engineer-General'. Assisting him were the 'Solicitors-General' Cobbold and Owen, and the 'Secretary-General' Size. Their force came face to face with Munro's men, 50 navvies led by his agent named Fryer, a man who had been involved in a similar skirmish with the Highway Board at Lavenham. This time Fryer was to be on the losing side, but he was able to put up a spirited defence.

Fryer, obviously relishing his new military career, stationed his men at the head of a cutting so that he could not be attacked from behind, then hurled a few oaths at his foes. After several struggles, the longshoremen made a successful assault and captured Fryer only for the navvies to attempt to retrieve him. Such was the battle over the custody of Fryer that for a time 'the luckless general seemed in imminent peril either of strangulation or dismemberment'. Cooke's men won in the end, and secured their aim of being able to 'lift' Fryer off the Railway Company's property.

Fryer was not to be put off by losing the first round and, collecting as many of his navvies as he could, he made a second stand at another cutting. This time his navvies proved less willing to fight, and he was again 'lifted' off the Railway's property. A third stand proved equally useless and at the end of the 'Battle of Bradfield' Furness was the contractor left in charge of the works.

No charges for assault or any other crime seem to have resulted from this struggle, which certainly broke several laws. It is interesting to compare how open to interpretation questions of 'law and order' appear to have been in Victorian Essex.

ASSAULT

❦ ◊ ❦

O NE of the arguments that modern media pundits like to put forward is that life has somehow become more violent since the rosy days of their youth. This is one of those cases of the mind choosing to forget the things it doesn't care to remember, for there is absolutely no evidence to suggest that life years ago was somehow less violent and turbulent than it is today. In fact daily life in Victorian Essex seems to have included a good deal of 'rough and tumble', quite a lot of it inspired by an excessive consumption of alcohol. There were literally thousands of cases during Victorian times that involved the magistrates in deciding who started the fight, who should shoulder the blame, and what punishment was fitting.

The most common factors in cases in which assault was involved were attempts to rob and the drinking of alcohol. In almost all cases where there was no attempt to steal something, it was alcohol that lay at the root of the assault. For much of the Victorian Age, alcohol was more freely available than it is now for there were few restrictions as to hours for the sale of drink and also a far larger number of inns and beerhouses. Such was the concern in Colchester about drunkenness and disorderly conduct, that the *Essex Standard* conducted an investigation to see how it compared to other towns; they found that in the year ending September 1865 there were 67 actions against persons for being drunk and disorderly in Colchester, compared to 104 in Cambridge and 80 in Norwich. As a ratio per thousand of population though, Cambridge emerged with 3.95, Colchester with 2.82 and Norwich with a mere 1.07. It was Gladstone who attempted to tighten up the alcohol situation with the Licensing Act, but it led to his defeat at the following election of 1874, in which he felt he had been 'borne down in a torrent of gin and beer'.

Chelmsford Petty Sessions for January 1839 show that a lot of people celebrated Christmas 1838 by getting too drunk and ending up in trouble. On 20th December 1838 Mr and Mrs Jonathan Perkins were in the tap room of the 'Rodney' at Little Baddow when three troublemakers came in. They were Joseph Lucking senior, Joseph Lucking junior (his son) and William Lucking. Mr and Mrs Perkins wisely went through into another room to finish their beer, but William Lucking followed them through and demanded some of Mrs Perkins' beer. She refused, so he trod on her toes. Mr Perkins intervened at this assault on his wife, but Joseph Lucking senior came in and knocked him back over a stool; then Joseph junior shoved him against a wall. By this time the Luckings were just getting into the mood of it, so Joseph senior held Perkins down whilst the others 'strip't and paid him'. At the trial it was alleged that Perkins had been so troubled by his experience that he had been virtually bedridden ever since.

The trial proved to be quite an amusing one. The defence tried to allege that Mrs Perkins was a powerful woman of Amazonian habits, and called two witnesses who testified that Mrs Perkins was more than a match for all the Luckings put together! The defence argued that it was Mrs Perkins who had started the trouble by hitting Joseph Lucking senior in the face; she had then turned the younger two out of the pub, knocking her own husband over in the process. It was alleged that she had then rolled up her sleeves and sworn to fight any man who dared to come near her!

The magistrate, a local clergyman, listened to all this impassively and then fined William Lucking 2s 6d; charges against the others were dismissed, Finally, 'The Rev. T. Brooksby advised Perkins in future to send for his beer and drink it by his cottage fire-side.'

Similar scenes were going on in Brentwood that Christmas. On Boxing Day 1838 Constable James Livermore was called to the *Swan Inn* to arrest a lad who had been causing trouble; as it was about 9pm it is a fair bet that drink had started the problems. The Constable arrived and arrested the lad, but was then set upon by a gang of navvies led by one James Evans. The boy was set free and the Constable was struck in the mouth as a late Christmas present from the navvies. 'Respectable persons' came to the rescue of the

Constable and Evans was given six months hard labour as a warning to other navvies of what to expect if they caused trouble. These attempts to 'liberate' people taken into custody were quite common, and it was often difficult for the Police to arrest anyone at a public house.

The Queen's Head in Chelmsford was the scene of another drunken assault in December 1850. William Buck went into the pub, picked up Thomas Kemp's beer, and took two large swigs from it. Kemp, not surprisingly, objected to this but Buck got very excited and struck him on the hand with a poker. The excitable Buck then started to beat his poor victim on the head. A pub servant, Martha Lanham, rushed in because of the noise and found Kemp flat out on the floor with an irate Buck standing over him, shouting 'I'll kill you'. Buck then tried to run away, but was soon caught. For all this he was fined only £1, showing clearly how lenient the treatment of violence could be.

One of the more serious assault cases was in Romford in December 1861, as a result of which four men were charged with 'murderously assaulting' the Police. Their trial excited a lot of interest on account of the hardened characters of the men: 'The prisoners were most determined looking men . . . One of the bludgeons used in the affray – a very formidable looking weapon – was produced.'

On the day of what we may almost call the 'Romford riot', there had been a robbery in the town and the Police were looking for the criminals. Trouble began when the Police went to the tap room of the *Compasses* in Romford High Street. There, William May attacked Constable Dawes by striking him on the head with a pewter quart pot, causing him to bleed. Other Police came to the Constable's assistance and something of a free-for-all broke out in the pub, but the troublemakers were able to escape. The police then pursued them to the *New Mill* public house where they were attacked with bludgeons and a hail of stones. The rioters shouted out, in the censored version recorded by the Victorian press, 'Stone the . . . , knock their . . . eyes out!' One rioter, Nevill, struck a Constable on the head with a bludgeon.

The riot very soon got out of control, and the Police tried to get the men from the local brewery, who were watching, to assist; all the brewery men promptly vanished however. Constable Parsloes was beaten insensible by the mob, which had grown in number, and the Police Inspector had to lock himself in the Police station for fear of being lynched or killed by the hail of stones and cobbles. Other officers sought shelter in the houses of more friendly local people.

After the riot had died down steps were taken to arrest the ringleaders but a large number of those involved were never brought to court. Four men were tried for assault and given sentences of between 15 months and 3 years penal servitude. This was basically an old-fashioned anti-Police riot inspired by drink.

Assault was also a frequent factor in robbery, especially where the footpad style of operation was involved. An essential ingredient of this was to disable your victim, and if the footpad was operating alone this could only really be done by physical violence. John Mayne, a hawker, was walking along the road near Tolleshunt d'Arcy early in 1862, though he was foolishly travelling alone at night. All of a sudden he was struck a crashing blow across the nose with a bludgeon, and fell to the ground. There he was further set upon, being battered about the head and receiving 14 scalp wounds. Mayne might well have been battered to death had the footsteps of someone approaching not scared off his assailant; also because of this he did not lose the £6 he was carrying. Mayne's attacker was clearly a fierce and experienced footpad, because he was never caught; all Mayne knew was that the man who had attacked him was 'a tall man with a tall hat'.

Royal Wedding Day in 1863 should have been an occasion for merry celebrations, but as ever some people got too drunk to remain happy. James Betts was a beerhouse keeper at Mistley, and spent most of the day quarrelling with his wife. Joseph Goss, one of the customers, got fed up with this display of bad temper and tried to stop the argument, but Betts threw some beer in his face. Goss struck back with a stick, but Betts was the stronger man and succeeded in pushing him out of the building, causing Goss to receive a head injury. Goss's son reported that his father was 'bleeding like a pig'. Betts was fined £1 for this assault and then immediately tried on another assault charge, this time against George Vincent; this also occurred in his beer-house, but was dismissed as Vincent's father couldn't be bothered to come to court to give evidence. It is a wonder that Betts managed to attract any customers to his beer-house!

Some people visited pubs for reasons more sinister than getting

Lock-ups, like this one at Chingford were common throughout the county. They were used mostly for overnight housing of drunks, vagrants and other trouble-makers.

drunk. It was an ideal place to spot possible candidates to steal from, as a drunk was easy prey; this sort of crime was known as 'bug-hunting'. In July 1863 William Abrahart and Ray Rushbrook were drinking together at a pub in Epping, with the latter getting into an intoxicated state. Abrahart followed Rushbrook out of the pub, and chose a convenient spot to attack him, knocking the drunken man into a ditch. He made off with Rushbrook's boots and handkerchief. The next day Abrahart's lodgings were raided and a pair of trousers covered with blood and mud were found. Abrahart was arrested, and later sentenced to 15 years in prison because of the severity of his assault on Rushbrook.

Some assaults seem to have had no reason other than malice. In October 1863 Thomas Whiting was walking past Chopping's Mill in Colchester when he was stopped by a soldier, the latter being accompanied by some women. The soldier, Charles Watson, hit Whiting with his fist and then cut him with a bayonet. Watson then went off, but Whiting was able to get his name from the women and went to the barracks to have him arrested. Watson escaped punishment though as no-one would testify against him other than Whiting.

Special events like fairs tended to attract heavy drinkers and thus were associated with trouble. Walter Richardson assaulted Augustus Sewell at Ingatestone fair in December 1869, for example, and was given 6 weeks in prison.

A more severe assault took place at the *Ship Inn* in Brightlingsea on 3rd March 1871. William Davis, a fisherman, was there with William Everitt; the latter was rather a poor man. Despite the lack of money they were drinking together and tossed for who should buy the next drink. Everitt lost, and Davis proceeded to taunt him, stating, 'Don't cry because you've lost a pot of beer; ain't you got any money?' Davis even alleged that Everitt's clothes hadn't been paid for. After a while Everitt lost his temper, and threw the beer in Davis' face. Davis appears not to have reacted to this at the time, for they both went through into another room where some dancing was going on, and stayed there until well past midnight. An hour and a half later Everitt went out of the pub into the yard 'for a necessary purpose', and Davis followed him. Out in the yard Davis assaulted Everitt and stabbed him 'in the private parts'. This attack had a drastic effect on Everitt, who was confined to bed for a month afterwards and claimed to have nearly died. Davis was given 5 years penal servitude.

Christmas seems to have been a busy time for publicans and Police officers. Robert Bragg of Halstead was arrested just after midnight for being drunk in the street at Halstead, on Christmas Day 1871. Bragg was carousing, swearing and trying to play a clarinet without much success. A Constable advised Bragg to go home, but Bragg disliked this and tried to hit the Constable. He then grabbed the officer's cape and refused to let go, causing it to tear. When brought before the Magistrates, Bragg's defence was that he ought to be allowed to play *Rule Britannia* on Christmas Day. They were not impressed, and fined him £2 for assaulting the Constable.

Some larger houses had their own brewhouse, especially at

farms where beer was prepared for the labourers. A lively scene took place in the brewhouse of an East Mersea home in March 1872. The house belonged to William Cockerell, who on the night in question had gone out to a dinner party leaving his children in the care of the nursemaid and the cook. This provided an excellent opportunity for the two young women, who promptly invited their boyfriends – Edward King and John Theobald – around for a romantic evening. All four were in the brewhouse together when, to their amazement, Cockerell jumped through the window. Edward King had been having a good time with the nursemaid, but suddenly found himself grabbed by the throat and lashed with a whip, before being dragged outside. In the yard King was struck in the face. Meanwhile Theobald, who had been with the cook, was able to escape through the window.

When brought before the magistrates Cockerell said that he was irate because his servants should have been looking after the children and because King was drinking his beer. King denied this. Cockerell was fined one shilling plus costs, a miserly amount which shows that the magistrates sympathised with him.

An unusual form of assault was that against yourself, for to attempt suicide was a criminal offence in Victorian Essex. As the century progressed, the enforcement of this law became noticeably less harsh. In January 1875, Kate Aldridge tried to kill herself with oxalic acid at Woodford. She did this she said because she was tired of life; her husband had gone away and had not sent her any money. However, she called the Police immediately and was given a powerful emetic. In court she was let off with a severe warning, but could have been sent to gaol.

A man who clearly found assault difficult to resist was Michael Quinlan. In late 1881 Quinlan was near Stratford when he came across Jason Rowe, an old man who was walking home. Quinlan asked him for money, but Rowe refused. Quinlan then knocked the old man down and kicked him in the head, leaving a 6 inch wound. Rowe was detained in the London Hospital for 5 weeks. Quinlan was arrested and remanded in custody, but during his time in prison he committed several more assaults on other prisoners. When he appeared in court the prison surgeon testified that Quinlan appeared to be barely sane, but it was also reported that he had five previous convictions. He was given 5 years penal servitude.

Two inveterate troublemakers seem to have been James and Walter Wright. When they were involved in a fracas at a pub in Hempstead in January 1882 they had already been summonsed to appear in court on another assault charge. On the occasion of the Hempstead trouble, they went to the pub with a hawker from Saffron Walden, but soon created such a disturbance that the landlord asked them to leave. They refused. Just to make the point clear, Walter Wright pointed a gun at the landlord and swore he would shoot him, but then assaulted the poor man with his gun barrel. The landlord tried to defend himself with a poker, but received a serious finger injury. PC Copping was sent for, but even he had difficulty coping with the Wright brothers. Eventually they were handcuffed and a horse and cart arranged so that the Constable could take them to the cells at Great Bardfield. This was not a successful journey, because at Great Sampford the brothers got out of the cart dragging the poor PC with them! Copping only managed to control them by using his staff liberally. Sergeant Skinner came to his assistance, but James Wright got away and it was only Walter who was delivered to the cells. Walter got 2 months hard labour.

An attempted suicide because of money worries occurred at Colchester in January 1882. John Vince was a young bricklayer, who for weeks agonised about spending £4-10-0d on a watch. He felt this was extravagant, but in the end bought the watch only to lose his job almost immediately. When his sister came home early one afternoon she found him hanging from a beam. She cut him down herself and he was revived. The magistrates treated this case leniently too, merely sending him to the workhouse so that he wouldn't have to worry about money!

Farm labourers were inclined to drink beer while working in the fields, especially in the summer when the dust off the crops made them very thirsty. This sometimes led to problems. In June 1886 Alfred Rolf and George Stock were working in the fields at Great Dunmow when a quarrel started. Stock slapped Rolf, who was working a scythe. Rolf hit back with what was in his hands – the scythe. He struck Stock across the shoulders, causing an 8 inch wound that lay bare one of his ribs. He was not able to work for weeks afterwards. Rolf was given three months hard labour as he had not premeditated his murderous assault.

A more organised form of assault was prize-fighting, which was particularly common on the fringes of London. The London sporting fraternity used to organise regular trips out into the countryside to prize fights, but these mostly occurred in Kent rather than Essex. There was a prize-fight at Walthamstow in May 1886 however, which involved George Mahoney and another fighter who was never caught. At about 10 o'clock in the morning, three or four Constables were walking along the Great Eastern Railway embankment when they saw a crowd gathered under the arches of the river Lea bridge. A ring had been formed, and two men were stripped to the waist. The crowd scattered, but the Police were able to arrest Mahoney and six others. Mahoney was clearly losing the fight, as his eyes had closed and he was suffering from head injuries. The fight was for a prize of £50, but Mahoney's prize was a few months in gaol.

THE POOR LAW

ONE Act of Parliament that had great significance for the
poor of Victorian Essex was the Poor Law Amendment
Act of 1834. Under this scheme poverty was to be eased
through 'indoor relief', which meant that all paupers could only
receive assistance inside the workhouse. The conditions that
should prevail in the workhouse, it was decreed, should be less
pleasant than the worst lifestyle in which gainfully-employed
people existed. The result of this was that a network of workhouses were established around the county, each serving a 'Union'
of parishes. The poor, though, hated the workhouse and would do
anything to avoid the loss of freedom and dignity that entering it
entailed. Many of the Essex workhouses still stand, several in use
as hospitals and old people's homes to this day.

The Early Days

The workhouse at Braintree opened in 1837, replacing old
poorhouses in Braintree and Bocking. The local Guardians soon
ran into problems over it, though, for they refused to appoint a
Chaplain and had a policy of letting the paupers out to church on
Sundays. This was contrary to the orders of the Poor Law Commissioners, who made complaints in 1838. The Braintree Guardians, though, were hopelessly divided between Anglican and
Nonconformist, and could not agree on a Chaplain. When the
Commissioners again complained in February 1839, they were
told that an average of 97 Braintree paupers went to church each
Sunday and there had only been a problem with one of them! This
was a blatant lie, for there were numerous occasions when paupers
went out to church and came back drunk; the usual punishment

for this was not being allowed out again for a while, though some persistent offenders were sent to the Magistrates.

Being let out on a Sunday allowed the paupers to get into all sorts of mischief. In February 1839 several paupers created a disturbance during the church service, one got into trouble for walking out halfway through, and several others never actually reached the church at all!

As the Braintree Guardians began to tighten up the regime, work was introduced. They decided to set the able-bodied paupers to work on oakum-picking; this is where old, tarry ropes have to be unpicked with the fingers, the fibres then being used to water-proof the decks of ships. When this idea was introduced in March 1839 ten paupers refused to do it; they were rewarded with between fourteen and twenty-one days in Springfield Gaol. The instruction to pick at least 3lbs of oakum per day was, however, reduced.

Most workhouses had their difficult cases, and in Braintree she was called Catherine Breed. Catherine and her child had been abandoned by her husband (which was an offence in itself) and, since she showed no desire to work, they ended up in the work-house. There she was a constant problem, being taken to the Magistrates several times for assault or disorderly conduct. Then the Guardians received an anonymous letter saying that Mr Breed had been seen at Downham Market in Norfolk, and a message was sent immediately to check if this was true. The local vicar replied to say that Breed had certainly been there, but he had disappeared again!

In August 1839 Catherine Breed was back in front of the Magistrates, having threatened the Matron of the workhouse. A month later she surprised the Guardians by declaring herself to be a Roman Catholic, and requesting that a priest be brought from Witham to attend to her spiritual needs.

Further efforts were made to get rid of her, interspersed with bouts of bad discipline. In April 1840 a Mr Ruggles Brice offered to 'liberate' her but then changed his mind, and a plan to get her to emigrate also failed. Her string of minor legal offences continued for years, including further charges of disorderly conduct, destruc-tion of a workhouse blanket and refusal to maintain herself when capable of doing so.

At Colchester they had similar problems with a character who

Rather than go into the workhouse, some women were prepared to risk prosecution by taking their children begging in the streets.

rejoiced under the name of William Whalebelly. In December 1837 he was given three months hard labour for absconding; this was his thirtieth time in court. Another workhouse inmate in trouble was John Alden, who falsely claimed that sheets on the beds had not been changed for 14 weeks. In April 1838 a gang of young boys each received two weeks detention for smashing the workhouse windows, and the following month two inmates received one and two weeks hard labour each for picking the locks in the workhouse!

However the worst trouble was in the Halstead Union area, reckoned to be the poorest in Essex. Over a period of fifteen months there was a series of eleven fires, many of which occurred on the premises of local Poor Law Guardians. Eventual damage was reckoned at over £10,000 and eventually Abraham Rayner was convicted of incendiarism. He was only caught after London police officers had investigated and after a £700 reward was offered. Several men were arrested in error, including Rayner's cousin. Perhaps the greatest irony of all was that Rayner helped to run the Halstead fire engine! He was sentenced to transportation for life.

Later Incidents

A number of paupers ended up in court because of their behaviour when inside the workhouse, but there were a number of other offences connected to the Poor Law that didn't necessarily involve the 'New Bastilles' as the poor called them. Two of these were the crime of deserting a family so as to leave it chargeable on the parish, and the crime of refusing to work and so becoming chargeable to the parish poor fund.

The latter offence trapped Jonathan Bradley early in 1839. He had been working for farmer Henry Marriage of Broomfield, but then refused to work unless supplied with two pints of beer per day. Marriage sacked Bradley, so that he had to go to the Chelmsford Union workhouse. He was later brought before the magistrates and charged with refusing to work, on which account he was found guilty. As the *Essex Standard* observed, 'The magistrates decided on giving him employment in the House of Correction for one month's hard labour'.

The offence of leaving your family chargeable to the parish was committed by John Unwin of Hadstock in July 1839. This was an

The Lexden and Winstree Union Workhouse, one of many in Essex introduced to house the destitute.

offence under the Vagrancy Act. The trial produced details of some complicated relationships in a small village. The Unwins had married 16 years before, but the marriage had not been a success and Mrs Unwin had left her husband after only about 5 months. She had then moved in with a wool-weaver named Stevens. After about 15 years together, Stevens had died and Unwin didn't see why he should have to support her. Mrs Unwin had even put on 'widow's weeds' when Stevens died. Unwin was let off, which seems a reasonable decision under the circumstances.

Some people, however reluctant, were forced into the workhouse by circumstances. On 25th June 1844 there was a blaze started by incendiarists at Stisted, near Braintree, in an area where unemployment and low wages had caused discontent. After the blaze, 19 paupers from the village marched to Braintree, where they paraded around the town and then requested to be admitted to the workhouse. The blaze seems to have been part of their protest, but no-one was arrested.

The workhouse itself was hardly a peaceful place and the paupers were expected to earn their keep through unpleasant tasks like unpicking oily ropes or working the treadmill. Some paupers refused to work, and were generally punished with a spell inside Chelmsford Gaol. There were also quite a few disciplinary problems in the workhouse, because by their very nature they tended to contain the more fractious elements of society. One such was James Rank, a Broomfield labourer, who was in the workhouse with his wife and 7 children. One day in January 1847 he caused a disturbance in the workhouse hall, so the Governor of the workhouse directed the porter to throw him out. Rank struck the porter on the head, for which he was given 14 days in prison. He was clearly a somewhat disturbed character as he had spent time in Witham asylum. The row that caused his problems on this occasion was with his wife.

People were occasionally released from the workhouse if they had a job to go to. Less usual was someone coming to the workhouse to seek someone to do a job for them. Mr Boreham of Childerditch went to his local workhouse, with his wife, to get a girl who could act as their servant; they chose young Sarah Atkins and took her back to their farm. Sarah was treated in a most cruel and heartless manner. On one occasion she was not allowed to go to bed until after midnight, then Mrs Boreham came upstairs and told her to undress. The farmer then came in and 'spanked her thirty times, if not more'. On another occasion Mrs Boreham stripped the girl naked and flogged her with a riding whip. Mr Boreham then hit her on the ear.

The girl was still technically in the care of the Poor Law Guardians, whose medical officer investigated the girl's allegations of ill-treatment. He found 52 stripe marks on her back where she had been flogged, and she was taken away from the Borehams.

An instance of a man leaving his wife and children 'on the parish' occurred at Great Burstead in 1851. William Gatt, a blacksmith, was sentenced to 21 days in prison as a result.

Charles Field from Ashdon did the same thing in 1862, though he only left two children behind. He absconded and was not caught, but was sentenced to 6 months hard labour in his absence.

The power of the workhouse Governor or 'Master' was considerable and was sometimes abused. The greatest temptation, though, was to fiddle the books and make a large profit out of running the workhouse at the expense of the Poor Law Guardians. Thomas Twose was in charge of the workhouse at Halstead and regularly ordered peas for feeding the inmates, but he sold these off to his own profit. The Guardians eventually discovered what was going on and alleged that he was guilty of 'systematic plunder'. The workhouse's 'Book of Entries' had not been kept properly, so Twose had been able to cream off 48 bushels of peas and 32 bushels of beans. The goods were passed on to Thomas King of the *Griffin Inn* for disposal. In fact Twose got the system working so well that the peas went straight to King and never came anywhere near the workhouse, though they were recorded in the books as having been fed to the paupers. Twose also stole furniture, cutlery and glass from the workhouse. At the trial in December 1865 King was acquitted, but Twose was given two years hard labour at Springfield Gaol. The Jury blamed the Guardians for being too lax in their duties.

Occasionally other people landed in trouble when trying to defraud the Poor Law Guardians. In 1882 the Relieving Officer of Tolleshunt d'Arcy whose job it was to administer the poor law money, was given 2 months hard labour after embezzling £2-4-0d of the funds. In 1886 Alfred Digby was charged with supplying adulterated milk to the workhouse; it was found to be 91% milk only. He was fined 40 shillings, with costs against him of £1-12-0d.

There was a whole catalogue of workhouse inmates who got into trouble by behaving badly. In Chelmsford in 1870 two inmates were given 21 days hard labour for 'assaulting and reviling' the Master and the cook. In Romford in 1874 John Taylor stole his workhouse clothes and got 18 months hard labour. Destroying the clothes that the workhouse had given to you was an offence as well, for which two vagrant labourers at the Stanway workhouse were given 14 days hard labour in 1890. Also in 1890 a woman in Halstead workhouse was given 21 days in prison for using filthy language to the workhouse doctor.

A more serious incident involved Christopher Bradley, an elderly inmate at Chelmsford who had been a constant source of trouble since being admitted in 1889. He had a violent temper and often smashed windows, until he got into severe trouble in January 1892. Bradley slept in the next bed to his victim, Robert Monk, aged 82. When the supervisor went out of the dormitory, Bradley leant across and struck Monk on the head with a chamber pot, causing a fractured skull and jaw. The supervisor returned to find the bedclothes and walls covered with blood. Monk died the

Many children earned a pittance in menial jobs like sweeping crossings to help themselves and their families keep out of the dreaded workhouse.

following day. Bradley was in Springfield Gaol when he heard the news, and was said to have been very sad, but he was really too old to punish in any effective manner.

In 1892 a blind tramp named Stephen Sergeant arrived in Braintree, having come from Newmarket in the company of a woman. He arrived on the Saturday and earned money by singing in the street, but on the Sunday he lost the woman and had to go to the workhouse as he had no-one to lead him about. There, in a fit of temper, he smashed twenty-four panes of glass in the tramps' ward. He was brought before the Magistrates who discharged him on condition he left the town.

The Poor Law Guardians of Saffron Walden Union were put in a difficult spot when their Relieving Officer was accused of indecency in 1892. Charles Johns, aged 70, was accused of having indecent relations with his 14 year old servant girl. The girl also claimed that Johns' 14 year old grandson was 'intimate' with her. She produced a diary recording the alleged events, but Johns was able to prove he was not at home on the alleged date of the offence. He was discharged.

UNUSUAL CRIMES

◈

THIS chapter looks at some crimes which are less familiar to today's readers. This includes some crimes that were common in Victorian times but are now rare, and some crimes that were unusual even in those days.

1. Poaching

Poaching was fairly common in Victorian times and had a long history. There was a certain amount of politics involved in it, for many agricultural workers considered that the poor man's rights had been hijacked when the local squires 'enclosed' the village commons and woodlands. Some continued to assert that they had the right to shoot for game on land which they believed morally belonged to the village in common whatever the law said. Perhaps it was also the desire to taste meat that inspired the poacher, so that the woods rang with nocturnal gun-shots and the landowners were forced to employ gamekeepers to catch the wily poachers.

Most 'poaching' involved game, though the offence of stealing the odd sheep or lamb was very similar to it. Punishments were also similar. Thus Thomas Ives and Isaac Sams of Hatfield Peverel were very similar to poachers, for they stole one ewe in 1838. The fact that two men stole only one animal shows that it was likely to be for their own personal consumption. Ives had been convicted 20 years earlier for stealing 8 bushels of wheat, so was transported for 15 years whilst Sams was sent away for 10.

There was a lot of poaching around the estate of Lord Braybrooke, who lived at Audley End. The struggles between the landowners and the poachers became quite bitter in this district, though it was of course the gamekeepers who stood the greatest risk of injury. Lord Braybrooke instructed his keepers not to carry firearms, believing this would lessen the chance of a fatal incident. On Christmas Eve, 1851, there was a large force of poachers out – presumably looking for their Christmas dinner. At Martin Wood on Braybrooke's estate, three keepers were out looking for poachers and came across a band of them. There was a 'fearful fight', with the keepers outnumbered two to one, with the poachers being described as 'desperate characters'. One of the poachers fired at a keeper, but only grazed his arm. Keeper Feetham managed to get one of the poachers into a ditch, but then needed help and the poachers were able to slip away.

Eventually arrested was Isaac Barker, who was out on Christmas Eve 1850 but not brought to court until March 1851. At his trial it was alleged that it had been Barker who fired the gun, being only two yards from the keeper at the time; apparently the shot caused the keeper's jacket to catch light! Barker had been out after pheasants, but had been involved in the struggle with Feetham, who had recognised him as they struggled in the ditch. He was sentenced to 7 years transportation.

At the same Assize another case involved a violent group of poachers from Stansted Mountfichet, who had attacked the keepers with bludgeons. They were given the same sentence.

The following year there was more trouble on Braybrooke's estate at Wenden. On this occasion a group of five young men were out doing some Christmas poaching, but the sound of their gunshots alerted the gamekeepers. The gamekeepers trailed them into a plantation and there caught up with them. A fight resulted and Will Osborn struck out at one of the keepers, who replied by knocking him down. Osborn was arrested but escaped on a legal technicality as they couldn't prove that he had been poaching.

Poaching also seems to have been common in the villages around Witham. In late 1863 there was an incident at Rivenhall Thicks as a result of which Henry Townes and Thomas Ager, both quite young men, were charged with shooting at gamekeeper William Murrells. The gamekeepers had found a snare in the Thicks and were keeping watch on it, knowing that the poachers would return to check it. After a cold and fruitless night of waiting, the keepers were stirred into action by the arrival of two men carrying guns at 6am. The keepers attempted to surprise them, but in the scramble guns were fired. Townes struck one

A group of Essex police at the end of the Victorian era.

keeper with the butt end of his rifle, then tried to choke him with his neckcloth. Murrells chased Ager, but the poacher turned and shot at him; his thick smock saved him from serious injury. In his defence Ager claimed that the trees had caught his rifle and caused it to go off, but both men were found guilty and sentenced to 5 years penal servitude.

Another incident in the district occurred at Great Braxted on 18th November 1872. It took place on the estate of Sir Thomas Western, the Lord Lieutenant of Essex, and a gamekeeper – Thomas Dudley – was killed. Dudley had been working on his own and, after the sound of gunshots, two other keepers rushed to the area where they knew he had been. They found him lying on the ground, shot through the thigh. He died later of his wounds. He had been shot from a range of about four yards.

The keepers knew who to suspect, and Police help was summoned from Witham. Sergeant Buck and other officers visited the houses of the suspects. Buck went to William Bundock's house at about midnight, and found quite a lot of evidence: wet and dirty clothes were lying about, with powder and shot in the jacket pockets, whilst there was a gun hidden under the bed. Bundock and two others were arrested and taken to Witham Police Station.

The Coroner decided to record a verdict of wilful murder, but at the trial the prosecution was unable to prove that the murder had been deliberate. Most of the poachers involved were of backward development, it being said of Bundock that '. . . he had a low, narrow forehead, and is evidently of a low intellectual type'. It was decided that the gun went off in the panic of being discovered, and so the three were punished with varying sentences of penal servitude.

There was more trouble on Lord Braybrooke's estate in November 1881, this time at Green's Wood near Littlebury. The keepers heard several shots at about 7pm and went into Green's Wood to listen. They heard more shots at about 9pm, then saw three men walking towards them; it was a bad night for poaching as there was a clear moon, and the keepers recognised two of the poachers. One of the keepers spoke out, and the men turned and fled, but the keeper had seen that one was carrying a gun and some pheasants.

Two of the poachers were a father and son, both called Jesse Webb. The Police were called out to investigate, but the pheasants were found abandoned in the countryside and still warm. Jesse Webb junior was arrested at his house – the policeman found him in bed, but there were wet mudprints on the stairs and the young man had a loaded gun in bed with him! However he was fined only £5, which suggests that someone had sympathy for him!

2. The Sea

As far as crime is concerned, the sea is usually associated with tales of smuggling. By the Victorian era though, the heyday of the smuggler had passed and smuggling cases were usually small affairs and quite lacking in the romantic spirit of the 18th century struggles against the Customs Officers. There was still a small smuggling trade in items like brandy which were heavily taxed, but it was small-scale in comparison to what had gone before. In 1862, for example, an elderly couple from Wrabness were found to have been supplying brandy to various persons in the district illegally. Customs men found several barrels of it at their home. They were fined £12-10-0d.

There was certainly nothing romantic about a case involving seafaring activities at Wivenhoe in 1851. There was quite a fishing trade there but not all the fish that were landed were sold.

Unwanted fish were left to lie around until they went putrid, and were then taken off to use as manure. Isaac Ladbrook got into trouble for leaving large quantities of putrid sprats on Wivenhoe quay. The result of this was a smell which caused a 'nuisance'. The Surveyor of the Parish, John Death, went to investigate and received a torrent of abuse from Ladbrook, who shook his fist in the Surveyor's face. Ladbrook was brought before the Magistrates and cautioned.

In late 1861 some Essex men were in severe trouble on a charge of 'wrecking', which was an offence against the Merchant Shipping Act. Basically, the unauthorised removal of any goods from a wrecked or abandoned vessel was prohibited. The incident involved the *Regina*, which was on its way from Kronstadt to London with a cargo of tallow in November 1861. The ship, which was a brig and had a home port at Whitby, was wrecked on the Middle Swin sands on 13th November. The crew were rescued by the *Effort*, which was in the vicinity, and taken to Whitstable in Kent – even though the *Regina* had been wrecked only 8 miles off the Essex coast. The cargo was worth about £17,000, so the Lloyd's agent soon put out from Whitstable to investigate, in the company of the *Regina*'s captain. When they got out to the Middle Swin sands they found the *Regina* surrounded by a number of fishing smacks, whose crews were plundering the cargo. The Lloyd's agent ordered them to stop, but they refused. Help was therefore summoned from Sheerness, and some Marines were able to assist in the capture of two of the smacks – the *Prima Donna* and the *Sarah*. These were taken to Sheerness and found to contain tallow stolen from the wreck. Six Brightlingsea seamen were charged in Kent with wrecking, and found guilty; they were each fined £100, a very sizeable sum.

In January 1862 the six convicted men appealed against the decision at the East Kent Quarter Sessions. Their defence argued that the event had taken place too far from the shore to be covered by the Merchant Shipping Act, but the appeal was dismissed

3. The Strange Case of 'Dummy'

Essex is famous for its connections with witchcraft, particularly in the period 1600–1700 when Matthew Hopkins from Manningtree became almost legendary as the 'Witchfinder General'. By the 19th century official attitudes were more enlightened so that people were no longer prosecuted for being witches. In fact most of the people who had been accused of witchcraft were simply 'outsiders' who became scapegoats for local troubles. Despite official attitudes, superstitions lived on and harmless old people were still accused of witchcraft by other villagers. A common way of testing for witchcraft had been 'swimming', whereby the suspect was thrown into water to see if they floated or sank. This was done in the celebrated Coggeshall witch case, as a result of which an old lady had sickened and died. By Victorian times this sort of thing was a criminal offence – if anyone was unofficially 'tried' and then died, then the perpetrators of the act could be brought to court.

This was the background to the 'Dummy' case that occurred in Sible Hedingham in 1863. The victim was a poor old man called 'Dummy', who could neither hear nor speak and who was reputed to be French. He lived in a hovel in the woods outside the village, and was treated with suspicion by the villagers. This sort of person was the 'classic' victim in witchtrials – an outsider, whom no-one knew much about, and who suffered some form of handicap or deformity.

In August 1863 a number of people gathered at the *Swan Inn* at Sible Hedingham, one of whom was Dummy. A woman there, Emma Smith, complained that the recurrent illness she was suffering from was Dummy's fault – he had bewitched her. Rumour had it that Dummy was involved in casting spells and telling fortunes, so he was a natural target for such accusations. Emma Smith tried to give Dummy some money in the hope that he would take the spell off her, but he declined the money.

It is easy to imagine that drink played a large part in the subsequent proceedings. Dummy went outside, where a crowd gathered as Emma Smith continued to try to persuade him to remove the spell. Exasperated, she then dragged the old man off to a nearby brook and pushed him in. Whether she did this in a deliberate attempt to 'swim' him, or whether it was just a malicious way of working out her frustration, is not clear. Samuel Stammers, a local carpenter, came to help Smith and together they pushed the poor old mute into the brook several times. When he tried to go home, Emma Smith assaulted him several times.

The soaking and the beating did Dummy no good at all, and he was taken to Halstead where he died almost exactly a month later. This put a very serious face on the case, since medical opinion was that Dummy had died as a result of his ill-treatment.

The Swan Inn at Sible Hedingham. Excessive consumption of alcohol played a large part in Essex's last case of witchcraft.

At the subsequent Assize, Smith and Stammers were charged with assaulting Dummy and causing his death, though they were lucky not to be charged with manslaughter. At the trial, Emma Smith made much of Dummy's reputation for witchcraft. She claimed that he had spat on her and her illness had resulted, which the doctors were powerless to cure. She also argued that the attack on Dummy had been conducted by virtually everyone at the *Swan*, and that there were several others more deserving of punishment than herself. Among them she accused Stammers, who she claimed had taken Dummy by the heels and thrown him into the water. They were both given 6 months hard labour.

4. The Brightlingsea Fraud Case

Fraud was relatively uncommon in Essex. The nearest that most local criminals got to it was 'coining' – the making of fake coins. There were outbursts of this in Colchester and Southend, but it was a difficult crime to get away with. The tell-tale moulds used in forging were the downfall of many an Essex coiner, since they could not be easily hidden if the Police raided a house.

More elaborate fraud was rare. One of the more major cases that affected Essex was of a criminal who had committed his frauds elsewhere, but who tried to 'go to ground' in Brightlingsea.

The young man concerned used the name Henry Williams during his Essex days, but his real name was Edwin Yates. He was a woolstapler by trade, and originated from Ross-on-Wye in Herefordshire. Through some scheme he managed to defraud the Gloucestershire Banking Company of £7,000, and then vanished. Detectives from Hereford and London were put onto the case, but they had to travel huge distances and eventually lost track of him. One detective trailed Yates to Southampton and then to Manchester, but Yates fled abroad. When he was eventually arrested he claimed to have been in France, Antwerp and Hamburg. He must have yearned for his home country though, for in December 1869 he arrived at Brightlingsea on a fishing smack from Dunkirk; he began a new life as Henry Williams.

The impression he made on Brightlingsea was a good one. He was said to have had an 'aristocratic appearance' and became a regular attender at the town's Methodist chapel where he set up a day school for local children. Perhaps using some of the stolen money, he opened a small stationery shop. He gave himself away, however, by rashly writing an anonymous letter to a friend in Hereford. The postmark betrayed that he was at Brightlingsea, and detectives arrived to hunt for him. They arrived at his school room to find the pupils there but no 'Williams', so they then hid in the inn opposite until he showed up. Then he was promptly arrested to the surprise of the local people. He was taken back to Hereford for trial.

5. The Railways and Crime

Perhaps because the railways were new they tended to attract the interest of over-curious persons, but certainly when trains came to Essex they seemed to be at the centre of a lot of crime. Some was the result of curiosity and some due to malice.

A combination of drink and curiosity seems to have been the case with John Thorogood, who got into trouble at Shenfield in 1840. The crew of a locomotive left their engine in steam and unattended when they went to get their supper, and a curious

Thorogood arrived to have a look at it. He seems to have been something of a railway enthusiast, for he had been ordered off railway property not long before. This time he clambered up onto the engine, though in an intoxicated state, and began interfering with the controls. When the locomotive lurched forward Thorogood lost his balance and fell off the footplate, leaving the engine to proceed off with no one at the controls. It knocked a carriage off the tracks and headed off into the countryside. The line to Colchester was not complete at this stage though, and the engine didn't get far before running out of track.

Thorogood was arrested and charged with setting an engine in motion so as to endanger life. Much was made of the great luck which caused the engine to head away from London – had it gone the other way disaster might have occurred. Thorogood was given six months in prison and a £5 fine.

When railway officials seemed to be responsible for a fatal accident they could be prosecuted; in practice this meant that engine-drivers in the early days of Essex railways were occasionally accused of manslaughter. These cases usually attracted great interest, especially as the local Eastern Counties Railway was quite notorious for the number of accidents it had had. In 1851 even *The Times* was forced to express an opinion, claiming that the ECR had 'killed Her Majesty's lieges by scores in the first year of its operations'.

A railway accident that ended up with a manslaughter prosecution occurred at Ingatestone in 1851. Driver Wilson was in charge of a Colchester to London luggage train and left Chelmsford just ahead of an 'up' London passenger train. Because of this he had to stop at Ingatestone and shunt into a siding to let the passenger train pass, but a derailed coal wagon blocked the points and Wilson got out. However, the stoker started the engine without the driver's permission, and the driver was crushed between the coal truck and the vehicles of his own train. The *Essex Standard* said 'So firmly was the poor fellow fixed that nearly twenty minutes elapsed before his body could be extricated, when life was found to be extinct, and from the nature of the injuries sustained it is thought death was instantaneous'.

The news was rushed to driver Wilson's wife, who was ill in bed. It was later said that she expired when told of his death. The stoker was tried for manslaughter but was found not guilty. This was the second case within the space of a month in which Eastern Counties staff had been acquitted on such a charge.

The case of Thompson v. Eastern Countries Railway in 1851 was most unusual, for Mr Thompson had decided to sue the ECR for wrongful imprisonment. The press, ever anxious to denigrate the ECR, saw a great opportunity in this story; after all, wasn't it the ECR that had been described by *The Times* as 'a living embodyment of folly, fraud, delusion, recklessness and suffering . . .'? Thompson had gone to Ilford station in November 1851 with the intention of travelling from there to London in a third class carriage. The Colchester to London train had arrived and Thompson had been misdirected into a second class carriage by the guard, who was in a hurry. The train was running ten minutes late so the guard, according to the *Essex Standard*, was 'off his guard'. At Stratford Thompson was stopped by a ticket inspector, who demanded 5d from him for travelling in the wrong class of carriage. Thompson only had 2½d on him. He was arrested by the station staff, taken to the local Police station, and kept in custody overnight. The following day he was fined 2s 6d plus costs by the magistrates. In order to pay this, and thus secure freedom, Thompson had to pawn his watch. Subsequently he managed to have the conviction overturned, and then gained £50 damages from the action brought in December 1851.

There were numerous attempts at vandalism against trains and a few more serious efforts to cause accidents. In June 1899 two small boys from Copford put 41 stones on the railway line, though it is unlikely that this was an attempt to derail the train. The driver of an 'up' train spotted the stones and reported the incident, which was one of several that day. The two boys were caught and promptly blamed each other. One was given 12 strokes of the birch and the other 6.

A railway employee who obviously had more than enough spare time was the Woodham Ferris stationmaster. When he arrived to take up his post in 1889 the station house had not been completed, and so he took up lodgings with a local farmer. In time-honoured fashion, the stationmaster and the farmer's wife became 'intimate', and it wasn't long before the farmer began to suspect. When he had been out for the day he returned to find that the sofa had been moved and that his wife appeared 'flushed'. On another occasion he noticed that the spare bedroom had been used whilst he himself had been asleep. He began divorce proceedings; the highlight of this for the local press was the number of children involved – the farmer's wife was mother to 9 and the stationmaster was father to 17! Though no-one in this episode was actually a criminal, divorce proceedings in Victorian times were often very complex legal affairs.

Essex had an interest in an unusual London case in January 1862. Mr W.E. Windham was the subject of an action in the Westminster Court of Exchequer for insanity, brought against him by his own relative, General Windham. The younger Windham appears to have had a great deal of money and not very much to do, and had amused himself by behaving in an extraordinary manner on the railways of East Anglia. He first came to the attention of Essex when an inspector of Colchester railway station was alerted by the wild blowing of a locomotive whistle even though the loco was stationary. When he investigated, he found that Windham was the culprit. The inspector 'came to the conclusion that he was short in his intellect'. On another occasion an engine-driver was fined for allowing Windham on the footplate between Colchester and Ipswich, the implication being that Windham had handled the controls. In Suffolk Windham made regular appearances on stations, dressed in railway uniform and blowing a guard's whistle. He had a number of friends on the railway staff, who he cultivated with champagne and sherry. A description emerged of one heavy drinking session in a guard's van. Windham also had a set of carriage keys which he used to lock and unlock the railway company's vehicles. All of this, the *Essex Standard* felt, helped to explain the number of accidents on the County's railways:

'Our readers, on seeing this evidence, how wild young men of property – and in this instance half idiot (at least) – are allowed to cause carriages to be locked for adulterous amours, and to act as guards and engine-drivers, will not be much at a loss to account for some of the many accidents and irregularities which from time to time have made the Eastern Counties Railway notorious.'

As a result of this behaviour General Windham had an action brought to have the young man declared to be a lunatic. At the trial it emerged that the young man had had an unhappy marriage

– he had married an immoral girl against the wishes of his father, and she had left him for another man. The trial was spectacularly expensive – estimates were that it cost £160 per hour. Windham junior escaped with his freedom however, for late in 1862 he was spotted in action as a 'guard' at Cambridge and Ely.

6. Other Unusual Crimes

We normally consider road traffic accidents to be part of the age of the motor car, but in fact there were quite often accidents even in the days when the horse and cart was the staple means of transport. Even though speeds were much lower, there were still occasional fatal accidents. One such occurred in Bocking in January 1839. Mr Poulton, the Bocking vet, had engaged a young girl named Charlotte Martin as a servant. On the fatal day his son went over to Baddow in a gig to collect the girl. They had just got

A type of crime now mercifully forgotten. A debtor is taken away to gaol.

back to Bocking, and were stopped at the door of Poulton's house, when a coal waggon driven by Thomas Halls of Toppesfield went by at a fast pace. The waggon caught the wheel of the gig, throwing both young Poulton and Charlotte Martin into the street. The back wheel of the coal waggon passed over Charlotte's neck and killed her instantly. There were two men in the waggon, but both ignored or did not see the accident and Constable Brown had to be despatched in pursuit. Halls was found to have been 'the worse for liquor' and the jury at the Coroner's court recorded a verdict of manslaughter against Halls.

The law in Victorian times was quite strict about a labourer's relationship to his master. Thus James Devall of Colchester was given 14 days hard labour for 'absenting himself from the service of his master' in January 1839.

A considerable nuisance to Colchester in 1839 was Mary Folly, an Irishwoman. She had first come to local attention when she had been taken to Lexden workhouse virtually dead, but she had made a very sudden recovery. She had explained that she was on her way to Norwich, so had been given two shillings to hasten her departure in that direction. She got no further than the vicinity of Colchester Castle where she took up residence to the distress of the local inhabitants. Her 'loud and piteous wailings of distress' caused the local people to summon the constable, who found her sitting near the gate 'giving vent to her sorrows in sonorous fashion'. She was taken before the Magistrates, who she told she was Irish even though she had told the people at Lexden that she was Scottish. The Magistrate then called her an imposter, as a result of which she '. . . indulged the Court with one of her characteristic howls, begging hard at the same time for mercy.' She was reprimanded by the Mayor and released on condition she left the town.

Church is not a place to associate with criminal activity, but there were legal requirements dating back to the time of Queen Elizabeth as to how to behave in Church, and if these were broken the Churchwardens could despatch the offenders to the Magistrates. John Taylor and William Chapman were a source of nuisance at Wivenhoe church, where the nuisance they made of themselves in the gallery there delayed the start of several services late in 1839. They called out to pretty girls in the congregation to come and sit on their knee, and laughed loudly when Rev. James

Ind stood in the pulpit. This sort of offence was normally punished with a small fine.

At the very end of 1846 Thomas Babbs, a labourer from Margaretting, was in trouble. He was charged with 'negligent conduct' as a result of having been far too long on a journey he was making for his employer – the cause of the delay being, inevitably, drink. He'd been sent to Chipping Ongar with a load of peas and had arrived there at about noon. He was still there at 5pm, even though he should have returned straight away, and did not get back to Margaretting until midnight. He was found by his employer's son, lying in the cart, a mile from the village. The son was convinced that Babbs was intoxicated, but at his trial Babbs argued on this point: 'He could not tell whether I was drunk or not because he did not see me on my feet.' This feeble defence convinced no-one, and Babbs was fined a day's pay plus costs of 11s 0d.

An amusing libel case was tried in Colchester in 1875, which resulted from years of arguing between two well-educated men. John Hampden, aged 54, of 'superior education but no job', was charged with defamatory libels against Alfred Wallace. He had accused Wallace of being a scoundrel, a thief, a swindler etc. Hampden openly admitted that he had accused Wallace of being these things for a period of over five years, but maintained that his charges were correct. The cause of this strong feeling between two men was an argument over whether or not the earth was flat! Hampden maintained that it was, and in 1870 had placed £500 stakes on proving it to Wallace with a test along 6 miles of the Bedford Level in the Fens. Hampden claimed that he had only lost the bet because Wallace cheated. The facts must have weighed heavily against Hampden when it came to court and, as he refused to give up the libelling, he was punished with twelve months in prison.

A charge that we don't hear much about today is 'causing and working a horse in an unfit state'. Inspector Rogers of The Hythe noticed this offence being committed by a coal merchant in 1882, the man's horse evidently being in severe discomfort. When the Inspector removed the saddle he found a sore the size of a five shilling piece, but the magistrates let the merchant off with a warning.

Arthur Howell was a skin dealer of Priory Street, Colchester. In

May 1880 he took over some premises in Bourne Pond Road, Colchester (now Bourne Road) and caused considerable discomfort to the local residents through the bad odour that resulted from his activities. Barrels delivered by the railway company contained animal entrails and seemed to be related to the stench, which could be smelled 100 yards away in Wimpole Lane. William Steggles, the Inspector of Nuisances, visited the premises in July 1881 and reported that 'there was a most fearful stench about the premises'. He visited again in November 1881 and found scrapings of entrails lying uncovered on a dungheap. Howell was clearly contravening health regulations and was brought to court. He agreed to heighten his chimney by 28ft and to improve the drainage.

In 1890 John Cutting, a builder from Bradfield, was summoned by the Tendring Vaccination Officer for not having had his daughter vaccinated. Costs of 10s 6d were awarded against him and the girl had to be vaccinated.

Study Notes

A lot of the material in this book can be used as local history material, either worth looking at in its own right or as a means of illustrating themes in the widely used GCSE courses in British Social & Economic History. Apart from directly covering the theme of crime and punishment, this book can be used to provide material dealing with topics like the position of women in society, the working of the New Poor Law, and the events of a mid-Victorian election campaign.

Study Guide
It is suggested that this book is best used to study various themes in Victorian society. The sections of the book which apply to each theme are indicated with their chapter numbers.

Motives for Crime: Derek Fraser, the noted social historian, has written that 'most nineteenth century crime was concerned with gain.' Consider whether this was true and compare the Victorian situation with that today: have things changed, and if so, why? First have a look at the summary of the Assize trials given in Chapter One; it has not been possible to print full details of each case, but how many look as though they may have been motivated by personal gain?
Assess the importance of the various motives found in this book:
Hunger – sections 3i, 3ii, 3iii, 4iv, 8, 9i
Revenge – 5
Economic Interests – 5, 8
Profit – 2i, 3i, 3ii, 3iii, 4iv, 9i
Personal Motives – 2i, 2ii

Punishment of Criminals: especially section 1, but consider the sentences given to other criminals mentioned throughout the book. Then consider the ways in which crimes were punished, comparing the penalties given to those whose crimes were against property and against persons. A useful comparison might be between burglary and assault. What do your conclusions suggest to you about Victorian values?

Maintenance of Public Order: 5, 6.
Why did public order break down so frequently? Essex was most notable for its rural disturbances (see Malcolm Baker's booklet, 'The Revolt of the Field') and for its election disturbances (see also the present author's article in 'Essex Countryside', Sept. 1986), but overall it suffered less than many other Counties of the period. A student with more available time might care to study the very low rate of convictions after arson attacks during the main periods of incendiarism: why was this so? What were current attitudes to the Police?

Crimes that have Vanished: Examine why some crimes that were common in the 1880s have now virtually disappeared. This may be due to decline of motive or more effective law enforcement, occasionally also due to changes in the law and also social change.
  Highway Robbery – 3i
  Sheep-stealing and poaching – 3ii, 9i
  Breach of Promise – 4i
  Offences against the Poor Law – 8

Women in Society: Examine the problems and disadvantages of women in the Victorian era. 2ix and 4 can be used to assess the reason why child murder and concealment of birth were such common crimes. Section 4 can be used to assess the position of women in society. 4iv deals with prostitution – why was it so common in Victorian society? Recommended background reading: 'The Dark Angel' by Fraser Harrison (Fontana).

Project Work
  This material easily lends itself to project work by pupils outside of school and can provide an easy starting point for the research of local history using contemporary sources. A project could, for example, study crime in Essex (or a part of it) over the course of a particular year. Most of the larger libraries and record offices have a collection of local newspapers, generally on microfilm; access to the material is thus very simple.

Index of Places

This index lists Essex place-names; some of the names given are no longer officially part of the County, having been affected by the numerous changes of boundaries that have taken place. Where a town or village has a name beginning with some prefix such as 'Great' or 'West', then it will be found under the second part of its name. Victorian spellings are used.

Index of People